IMPROVING
ACHIEVEMENT
in
Low-Performing Schools

T0354187

IMPROVING ACHIEVEMENT
in
Low-Performing Schools

Key
Results
for
School
Leaders

Randolph E. Ward
Mary Ann Burke, Editor

CORWIN PRESS
A Sage Publications Company
Thousand Oaks, California

For information:

Corwin Press
A Sage Publications Company
2455 Teller Road
Thousand Oaks, California 91320
www.corwinpress.com

Sage Publications Ltd.
1 Oliver's Yard
55 City Road
London EC1Y 1SP
United Kingdom

Sage Publications India Pvt. Ltd.
B-42, Panchsheel Enclave
Post Box 4109
New Delhi 110017 India

Library of Congress Cataloging-in-Publication Data

Ward, Randolph E.
Improving achievement in low-performing schools: Key results for school leaders / Randolph E. Ward, author; Mary Ann Burke, editor.
    p. cm.
Includes bibliographical references and index.
ISBN 0-7619-3173-2 (cloth) — ISBN 0-7619-3174-0 (pbk.)
    1. School improvement programs. 2. Academic achievement.
3. Educational leadership. I. Burke, Mary Ann. II. Title.
LB2822.8.W27 2004
371.2—dc22   2003019511

04   05   06   07   10   9   8   7   6   5   4   3   2   1

Acquisitions Editor:	Robert D. Clouse
Editorial Assistant:	Jingle Vea
Production Editor:	Diane S. Foster
Copy Editor:	Stacey Shimizu
Typesetter:	C&M Digitals (P) Ltd.
Proofreader:	Mary Meagher
Indexer:	Juniee Oneida
Cover Designer:	Michael Dubowe

Contents

Introduction

As more states are developing accountability systems and encountering low-performing schools in crisis, schools and school districts are scrambling to identify comprehensive and innovative school site and districtwide management practices that respond to the multiple challenges and urban realities of student academic achievement. After becoming the fifth in a series of state-appointed administrators for the Compton Unified School District (CUSD) in 1996, Randolph Ward effectively restored the fiscal and academic responsibility to CUSD in 2001. The school district was $20 million in debt and over several decades had consistently the lowest test scores in California. The primarily Latino–African American school community was plagued with racial tensions, gang warfare, crime, and poverty, and up to 50% of students attending some of the districts schools lived in foster care or with other family members.

Under a key results reform process created by Dr. Ward, CUSD and other national public schools have accomplished the following outcomes:

1. Improved student achievement in the core subjects.

2. Aligned teaching and learning with student performance.

3. Linked professional development for all staff to the goals for students.

4. Created safe, clean, and secure school facilities.

5. Forged stronger linkages with parents, families, and the community.

6. Increased management effectiveness, efficiency, and accountability.

ORGANIZATION OF THE BOOK

This book describes six steps utilized by CUSD and other national schools struggling to overcome low performance. Each step provides a key results reform strategy with countless examples on how multistressed, low-performing schools can overcome obstacles to respond to the unique learning needs of students and adults. It is commonly recognized in education circles that principals and teacher-leaders know what to do to fix failing schools. It's not rocket science; what has been lacking is the will to do it comprehensively.

The leadership and reform process described in this book provides a support mechanism that can serve a school or school district experiencing any sort of academic or management crisis. The mission of the key results accountability process is to institute and document successful reform practices that address the multiple challenges facing low-performing schools. The reform process has the capacity to effectively implement appropriate action plans that reach and exceed a school's required growth results. This survival guide clearly facilitates a school's and a school system's ability to thrive by providing ample worksheets for central office personnel, school site principals, and teacher-leaders to help them create key results strategies that address their school community's individualized needs.

Step 1 describes an effective process for creating a school culture that will support school site leadership, empowerment, and key results accountability by building relationships with diverse stakeholders.

Step 2 defines how key stakeholders can support ongoing growth and build the internal relationships of district office administrators and principals teaming together for the common good of all students.

Step 3 provides an overview of how school principals and teacher-leaders can create a key results accountability process with corrective action plans and specific lessons that can have a direct impact on classroom instruction, teacher recruitment, staff development, and results-based teacher evaluation.

Step 4 describes trailblazing initiatives that guarantee student success, including motivational attendance programs, an accelerated learning program, an extended school-year program, and a curriculum alignment backloading process.

Step 5 summarizes effective parent and community involvement activities that can provide schools and districts with the support required to overcome low-performing school challenges and to maintain open communication to respond to ongoing community concerns.

Step 6 highlights effective business practices that schools and districts can utilize to effectively leverage adequate resources for diverse student needs.

The Conclusion discusses how these six reform steps can be sustained over time.

The Resource section describes the Results-Based Intervention for School Efficacy (RISE) project that is currently being used to respond to the complex needs of low-performing schools. In response to the No Child Left Behind initiative, RISE uses a crisis response team approach to facilitate the implementation of a corrective action plan and measures benchmark progress through a key results recovery matrix in urban school districts in California and in other large urban cities across the nation.

Acknowledgments

This book represents over 25 years of field research in low-performing schools and urban communities. By merging the expertise of highly motivated school principals, teacher-leaders, and district office staff, this book provides readers with an effective school reform accountability process that will increase a school site's and district's overall student achievement and business practices. This work represents the contributions of many urban leaders. I want to thank the following:

- My wife, the other doctor in the house, for her support and belief in our ability to succeed where so many had previously faltered.
- Delaine Eastin, the California State Superintendent and my boss, for her consistent support of my many difficult decisions.
- Mary Ann Burke for building internal partnerships around resources and for helping write this book.
- The LaVonne Johnson, Jackie Cochran, and Jamaiia Bond trio for their hard work and dedication to implement our initiatives, which improved learning opportunities for our students.
- Lois Hale, the teachers' union president, for working with me to create a team to get the results that we all so much wanted and deserved.
- Susan Stuart, our lobbyist, for going above and beyond in helping us garner resources and respect in Sacramento.

- Tom Henry, the executive director of the Fiscal Crisis and Management Assistance Team (FCMAT), for his support and expert assessment of our progress.
- Board members Patillo, Sanchez, and Woods for their undaunted support and desire to do what is best for our students.
- CUSD principals, who deserve much of the credit for our success. Without their willingness to learn and make a difference, there would be no success.
- Ari Swiller, a friend and Yucaipa business partner, for always being there when we need him, whether for financial or people resources.
- Steve Chesser, a Boeing business partner, for stepping up to the plate every year to help raise the achievement bar with funding to enhance afterschool and Saturday academies.
- Tim White and Javetta Robinson, who, when we called, answered in a big way. Thanks for coming to Compton and making a difference.
- The California Legislature and Governor's Office for supporting our efforts over five years.
- Dr. Carl Cohn and the Long Beach Unified School District for loaning staff and expertise to CUSD and never asking for anything in return. Your actions speak to your belief that all children can learn.
- The California Highway Patrol Dignitary Protection Unit for the many hours we worked together day and night. Your professionalism under very difficult circumstances is appreciated.

Corwin Press gratefully acknowledge the contributions of the following reviewers:

Cynthia A. Eliser
Principal
Raceland Lower Elementary School
Raceland, LA

Reginald Mayo
Superintendent
New Haven Public Schools
New Haven, CT

Lee F. Olsen
Educational Consultant
Bellingham, WA

Janet Williams
Deputy Superintendent for Cluster & School Leaders
Boston Public Schools
Boston, MA

About the Author

 **Randolph E. Ward's** teaching career spans more than two decades. Fluent in Spanish and English, he has been a teacher in schools in North and South America, including two one-year stints in Colombia and Venezuela. Before becoming the fifth state-appointed administrator for the Compton Unified School District (CUSD) in 1996, Dr. Ward was an elementary school principal and an area superintendent for the Long Beach Unified School District.

After a 10-year state takeover, Dr. Ward is credited with restoring fiscal and academic responsibility to CUSD, a school district that was $20 million in debt and had the lowest test scores in California. Under his leadership, the district's infrastructure was rebuilt from the ground up in order to build the capacity for student achievement districtwide and ultimately increase test scores over four consecutive years. Focusing on student achievement, accountability, and safety, he instituted corrective reading, accelerated learning classrooms for retained students, an extended school year, and an all-day primary learning program, as well as many other academic improvement programs. In 2002, 84% of Compton's schools improved their Academic Performance Index scores, and the percentage of black males graduating from Compton's high schools with the required University of California and California State College required courses exceeded the state's average.

Dr. Ward trimmed administrative overhead, forged new alliances with the community and district unions, authorized tens of millions of dollars in emergency school repairs, completed a multimillion-dollar facilities modernization and technology infrastructure project, and developed and implemented a Master Facilities Plan. In 2001, CUSD made history by becoming the first state takeover to repay its bankruptcy loan.

To fight grade inflation, Dr. Ward introduced a standardized grading program that relied on course content, writing rubrics, and standards-based assessments. Under his tutelage, staff and student attendance increased, high school graduation rates rose, college enrollments skyrocketed, advanced placement courses vastly expanded, community involvement improved, and the California Achievement Test (CAT5) and Stanford 9 Test scores improved continuously. School crime rates plunged dramatically because of such initiatives as school community policing, school site parent safety committees, the We-Tip hotline, mandatory school uniforms in K–8, zero-tolerance for weapons, and the use of enhanced alarm technology throughout the schools in the district.

Dr. Ward's nationally recognized, environmentally based school facilities grading program met with so much success that its criteria was expanded to include elements related to academic and instructional site-based programs. His inclusive approach and collaborative leadership style has taken administrators and staff, schools and parents, and the Black and Latino communities to new levels of cooperation and achievement.

Dr. Ward has a B.S. in early childhood education from Tufts University, a master's degree in school leadership from Harvard and a master's degree in educational administration from the University of Massachusetts, Boston. He also has an Ed.D. in policy, planning, and administration from the University of Southern California.

About the Editor

 **Mary Ann Burke** is an Adjunct Lecturer in Systematic Planning and Grantwriting for the School of Education at California State University, Sacramento. She is also an Adjunct Assistant Professor in the Rossier School of Education at the University of Southern California specializing in resource development for education. Dr. Burke has provided administrative program development, grantwriting, and assessment support to various Los Angeles County urban school districts, charter schools, and community-based organizations. During the last three years, she has assisted various school districts and community agencies in securing over $100 million in educational and social service programs and community development grant funding.

Dr. Burke is the former Director-Grantwriter for the Compton Unified School District. She was also the initial director of the Community Partnership Coalition VISTA Project sponsored by Fenton Avenue Charter School, which recruits and trains parents and community volunteers to serve as mentors and tutors in the classroom. She is coauthor of *Recruiting Volunteers, Creative Fundraising, Developing Community-Empowered Schools,* and *Leveraging Resources for Student Success: How School Leaders Build Equity,* and the author of *Simplified Grantwriting.*

1

Defining the School's Culture

A school's culture can be defined as the traditions, beliefs, policies, and norms within a school that can be shaped, enhanced, and maintained through the school's principal and teacher-leaders (Short & Greer, 1997). An effective process for improving a school culture includes empowering diverse stakeholders to rebuild relationships that will instill a staff's commitment to support student success in highly challenged school communities. When a school district or site has been challenged for its lack of performance, a survival culture permeates every dimension of the organization. Primary beliefs of the school staff focus on job security and basic survival. To create a new culture of change, school principals and teacher-leaders must focus on an overall organizational transformation that includes the following successful practices:

- Defining the role of the school principal, teacher, and school community through open communication and academic growth activities that can best serve the needs of a particular school community.
- Scheduling effective communication mechanisms, such as staff lunchroom visits, department forums, staff meeting pop-ins, and all-district personnel rallies.

- Sharing successes through employee union newsletters, internal correspondence, and community relations that breed further successes for diverse student populations.
- Visualizing schoolwide and classroom goals that support the goals of a school site and district to generate key results and offering staff development training that supports these results.

When working to change school culture for low-performing schools, principals and teacher-leaders must first consider the basic needs of their staff and their students. The school leaders must evaluate the social and environmental contexts of a school's practices to define the existing school staff's culture and norms when working with students (Forester, 1996). Additionally, staff members and students should not feel monitored, and the feelings of individual teachers and students must be acknowledged.

The student should be the centerpiece of defining a school's culture, because the student is the chief client served by the educational profession (Englert, 1993). When a school's culture can be reformed to support the assumption that all students have the capacity to learn and achieve, the school principal and teacher-leaders can modify previously held beliefs about how students learn and create new strategies to help low-performing students become successful (Burke, Baca, Picus, & Jones, 2003). Examples of how a school's principals, staff, and supporting school district can nurture high-performing schools and students include the following:

- School staff development and districtwide staff convention themes can be developed that focus on achievement (e.g., Everybody Counts Everyday, T.E.A.M.—Together, Everybody Achieves More).
- A school board and school site policy revision can include input from staff, board members, and the community.

- Standards of attendance can be central in all school reform initiatives, and teacher accountability should be paramount.
- School principals can instill the belief in all stakeholders that failure is not an option: It's only a nagging possibility that keeps school staff focused.
- School principals should watch their thoughts, words, actions, habits, and character, because they become their destiny.

UNDERSTANDING ATTITUDE DEFINED BY ACTIONS

A school community attitude is defined by those actions that support achievement. An effective school and community relations program requires ongoing two-way communication within that school community. By being aware of the school community's perceptions of the school, the school principal and teacher-leaders can (a) deal more effectively with misconceptions when they arise; (b) eradicate racial and economic disparities for students; and (c) reengage parents and community members into the unique learning needs of their student community (Oakes, Quartz, Ryan, & Lipton, 2000).

Reading the pulse of the community and forming effective partnerships with diverse community members requires the development of a proactive community relations program at the school. Effective community relations programs utilize community partners in their school reform efforts for overall problem solving, resource development, school-based and classroom monitoring of reform initiatives, and creating a seamless delivery of educational support services. Examples of effective school and district-based community relations strategies with diverse school community stakeholders include:

- Scheduling public board meetings at schools that incorporate staff and achievement recognition programs.

- Organizing brown bag lunches at schools to meet staff, share the school's vision and priorities, and discuss challenges, successes, needs, and questions.
- Providing community forums throughout the year at diverse geographical sites in the school community and presenting them at different times and in diverse languages.
- Convening whole-department meetings with district staff groups.
- Requiring a staff and community textbook account-ability committee to oversee the purchase and bar coding of textbooks.
- Organizing school-site beautification days with district office support.
- Hiring school counselors and security assistants to sup-port a healthy and secure learning environment.
- Creating maintenance strike teams at schools to provide immediate physical improvements.
- Organizing human relations camps for high school students.
- Analyzing leadership and learning survey data col-lected from principals and teachers to support district office decision making.
- Sharing successes through union newsletters and memos to staff.
- Using the media to document successes and build over-all school community morale.
- Interviewing the school principal and teachers and publishing stories about past successes in the classroom that correlate to success schoolwide.

Scheduling Effective Communication Mechanisms

An effective school-based community relations program should include ongoing publications produced by the school about critical school issues, newsletters, press releases, quarterly community forums, planned culturally sensitive community celebrations, awards ceremonies and testimonials, volunteer recognition events, and community partner celebrations.

At the school-site level, an effective community relations school staff member should be able to (a) interpret the school board policies to the school community; (b) serve as a source of information for the school community; (c) inform the school staff about community concerns and opinions; (d) create ongoing internal and external written communications; (e) create crisis management plans; and (f) provide ongoing schoolwide inservice trainings for all school personnel (Fiore, 2002).

Each activity that the public relations staff member maintains and develops should be organized on a predetermined timeline. For example, the parent handbook for each school year should be created in the early summer and mailed to parents as part of the back-to-school mailing in August. Press releases should be organized around the school calendar of events and key recognition activities. Form 1.1 provides a community relations workplan that can be used by a school site in planning appropriate community relations activities.

Form 1.1   Community Relations Workplan

Directions: The school-site public relations staff member and school personnel should complete the planning table with appropriate community relations activities and timeline for the school year.

Type of Activity	Activity Description	Timeline
Standard school-site publication (e.g., school-site parent handbook, community resource guide)		
School newsletter (e.g., school community news, student successes, new community partner contributions)		

(Continued)

Form 1.1   (Continued)

Type of Activity	Activity Description	Timeline
Press releases (e.g., test score results, events, grant program awards, student achievement)		
Quarterly forums (e.g., state and district standards, curricular choices to support state standards, student assessment instruments, student achievement)		
Cultural community celebrations (e.g., Martin Luther King Day, Cinco de Mayo)		
Awards ceremonies and testimonials (e.g., student achievement, school recognitions, guest speakers, legislator visits)		
Volunteer recognition events (e.g., thank-you lunches, volunteer play days with family, volunteer development programs, volunteer recruitment orientations)		
Community partner celebrations (e.g., community partner recognition events for adopt-a-school programs; event sponsorships; book, equipment, and supply donations; staff support and training donations)		
Other:		
Other:		
Other:		

2

Gatekeeping by the Central Office

Administrators and
Principals Teaming Together

Educational programs can be developed and promoted by key stakeholders to support the ongoing growth and internal relationships between district office administrators and principals. School principals and teacher-leaders can create a school culture that supports the district's goals for student achievement and expects the same standards for all students. These internal partnerships must focus on (a) improving student achievement in the core subjects; (b) aligning teaching and learning with student performance; (c) linking professional development for all staff to the goals for students; (d) providing safe, clean, and secure school facilities; (e) increasing management effectiveness, efficiency, and accountability; and (f) forging stronger linkages with parents, families, and the community.

Central office personnel and principal partnerships can also be developed through interactions with regulatory organizations, data-driven decision making, a staff leadership team's key results, convocations, high school student

7

leadership summits, and school-site visitation teams that use results measurements with a program-improvement approach to self-management.

Defining a School's Culture to Support Achievement Goals

A school's culture includes its traditions, beliefs, policies, and norms. These can best be modified by making visible and philosophical changes in the school's structure and processes (Short & Greer, 1997). When a school culture supports the assumption that all students have the capacity to learn, that school's community has the freedom to modify previously held beliefs. Beliefs that affect a school's culture and facilitate a learning community for all students include the following:

- All students must reach benchmarked standards of achievement. No exceptions! No excuses!
- The standards must be the same for all students.
- The contribution to student performance is the only criterion for judging the merit of any educational activity.
- Assessment systems, the curriculum, the entire instructional program, the professional development program, and the accountability system must be linked at every level to the academic standards for student achievement.
- Good instruction is important, but it is not enough. Each student needs to know that the school and district staffs care about him or her and that his or her success is achievable and important.
- The entire school community must be involved and organized to support all students.
- School and district support staff must provide high-performance and customer-friendly workplaces.
- A school staff must be provided with the freedom, training, and motivation to make informed decisions as capable employees who are then held accountable for the results of their work.

Based on the belief that all students can learn and increase their academic achievement, the school principal must focus on the following six critical school reform outcomes:

1. Improving student achievement in the core subjects.

2. Aligning teaching and learning with student performance.

3. Linking professional development for all staff to the goals for students.

4. Providing safe, clean, and secure school facilities.

5. Forging stronger linkages with parents, families, and the community.

6. Increasing management effectiveness, efficiency, and accountability.

The school principal and teacher-leaders can establish benchmarked learning expectations with accountability using systemwide and state-mandated assessments in reading, writing, and math. Primary students can be assessed in phonics, phonemic awareness, spelling, and sight word knowledge. Assessments can align state standards and a grade-level curriculum or instruction. Assessment templates and spreadsheets can be constructed to track student growth on a quarterly basis with individual teacher reflections and analysis. Student overall performance data can be compared to the state standards using classroom-based, district, and standardized assessments. Strategies that enhance student performance include the following:

- Assigning a set amount of homework per night, commensurate with age and accompanied by a program of parent coaching to enforce homework completion.
- Offering afterschool homework assistance.
- Making regular achievement recognition phone calls.

- Enforcing strict attendance standards, with morning phone calls to the homes of all absent students, purchased alarm clocks, and home visitations as needed.
- Mandatory school uniforms, with loaner uniforms available on school sites with changing rooms and laundry facilities.
- Using student portfolios to assist teacher conferencing with parents and students while teaching students how to monitor their own learning.
- Offering differentiated instruction and a variety of accelerated learning opportunities for low-performing students.
- Facilitating student participation in career-development field trips, university tours, career weeks, and Upward Bound or Gear-Up Programs to promote higher education.

Instructional leadership and accountability can be achieved for teachers by evaluating the merit of all classroom academic activities based on their contribution to student performance. School principals and teacher-leaders can continuously analyze, adjust, and improve their teaching practices and educational environment based on school-site data collection. Teacher accountability strategies include:

- Posting individual classroom and school-site improvement plans in offices and classrooms.
- Using all support staff for daily classroom visitations.
- Requiring daily learning objectives to be posted in the classroom.
- Requiring teachers to develop weekly curriculum objectives that are matched to students' needs. Principals can provide feedback on weekly objectives.
- Requiring bimonthly classroom assessments of curriculum objectives, which will be evaluated by teachers and school-site principals to determine the next steps for teaching effectiveness.

- Requiring quarterly spreadsheets of schoolwide assessments with teacher analysis or reflections.
- Requiring analysis of student work samples during grade-level collaboration meetings.
- Establishing weekly grade-level meetings in which teachers debrief on in-class visitations and new-teacher support.
- Establishing weekly teacher intervention meetings in which teachers debrief on at-risk students and determine appropriate interventions.

The school principal's assessment process should include an analysis of the school improvement plan; an examination of student achievement data; a comparison of student work related to the state standards in reading, language, and math; an audit of the curriculum and instructional strategies used to increase achievement; an examination of the status of the present level and type of parent, community, business, and university support; a budget analysis for optimal leveraging of resources; and facility and personnel management reviews.

The principal can collaborate with teachers to develop a school improvement plan and then map individual teacher's contributions and deliverables to that plan. The principal must monitor the classroom instructional program on a daily basis, with formal teacher assessments provided each semester. Teacher assessments can include classroom observations, individual meetings, and an analysis of classroom test scores. Teachers can also be coached on individual professional development and career plans. These holistic student and teacher accountability strategies can foster a culture of schoolwide accountability.

Professional development activities should provide teachers with opportunities to discuss, challenge, and learn from their colleagues in structured sessions. Sessions can be scheduled as summer new-teacher preparation institutes, bimonthly new-teacher trainings, bimonthly grade-level collaborations, monthly site staff management sessions, and professional development weeks. Professional development activities can include:

- Integrated day-to-day teaching utilizing various curriculum strategies.
- Modeling, coaching, and explicit feedback sessions.
- Reflections on new content guaranteeing that teachers understand the theory underlying the skills and knowledge given.
- Participation in the comprehensive reform process that focuses on continuous progress in student achievement and school improvement.
- Ongoing support and follow-up for continuous learning opportunities.
- Training on the reading process, including phonetic knowledge, articulation, phonology, orthography, morphology, comprehension, active participation, and English language development strategies.
- Training on a Key Results Classroom Quality Indicator Matrix that provides staff and school leaders with an assessment matrix for classroom visitations based on promising instructional practices, including effective lesson delivery, writing assessments, a student-centered environment, quality lesson plans, available instructional materials, test prep, safety nets, protection of instruction, and attendance.

A leadership coaching program can include (a) results-based classroom visitations and action-oriented monitoring; (b) English language learner compliance and quality instruction; (c) special education prereferral interventions and preventive strategies that work; (d) training and program development to help parents and the school community act as partners; (e) core academic standards; (f) school finance, facility, and personnel management; (g) alignment of curriculum and instructional materials; (h) alignment of student learning expectations to state academic standards; and (i) creation of assessment instruments, data, and school management technologies to improve pupil performance (English, 1992; Reeves, 2000).

Low-performing schools and school districts typically may have to comply with various regulatory teams, including the state's Fiscal Crisis and Management Assistance Team (FCMAT), the American Civil Liberties Union (ACLU), and the Office of Civil Rights (OCR) once they have been identified with low test scores, financial problems, and racial or ethnic tensions. Once a school or district has reached this crisis level, the school or district's whole culture must change to focus on student achievement through accountability.

School change should involve the students being served. High school and middle school students and student advisors can meet together through leadership summits to evaluate how their individual and district schools are academically performing. After an assessment of school-site and district data, student leaders can consider what they can programmatically do to overcome school-site obstacles for student achievement. Obstacles that can be corrected include (a) decreasing racial tension among students by forming human relations clubs at the school sites, (b) increasing student achievement by creating afterschool homework clubs, and (c) increasing school pride by organizing spirit events.

The school site can increase its overall ability to change its culture through participation in key results visitations. A districtwide or site-based key results visitation team can rate a school's facilities and instruction on a scale of A to F (Murphy, 2000). School facility and instruction grades can be posted in school buildings in the same way ratings are posted on various restaurants regarding the quality of the food, service, and facility upkeep. Added ratings can be established on (a) the availability of textbooks and instructional materials, audiovisual equipment, and technology in the classroom; (b) the presence of certificated teachers in the classrooms who demonstrate effective teaching strategies in student-centered environments; and (c) a schoolwide test preparation plan being implemented in classrooms that actively involves students in developing test readiness skills.

Key results regulatory teams can include district office and school-site administrators at all administrative levels, curriculum specialists, mentor teachers, support staff, and parent volunteers. The key results regulatory teams must be trained in how to adequately observe classroom teachers and school-site administrators while working with students using the key results indicators rating sheet. Site visitation teams should be trained in (a) how teachers can be rated in their lesson delivery, (b) how the classroom and school libraries are equipped and utilized, (c) how the school is implementing a writing assessment, (d) how lesson plans are designed, (e) the quality of the physical environment and whether it is student centered, (f) the availability of instructional materials, (g) the usage of a test preparation plan in the classroom, (h) the use of safety nets for at-risk students, (i) the use of safety nets for exceptional students, and (j) the protection of time used by teachers for instruction (Compton Unified School District School Operations, 2000). Ideally, the same classroom visitation team should visit the same teachers at least twice a year, unless a teacher or school demonstrates a need for more frequent assessments based on a corrective action plan.

After a school receives feedback from a key results visitation, the school will receive a final weighted score on the 10 items listed above (Compton Unified School District School Operations, 2000). Once weighted scores are tabulated on each key indicator, the indicator is graded for the school using the following scale (Compton Unified School District Research, Evaluation, and Assessment, 2001):

- 100–90 = A
- 89–80 = B
- 79–70 = C
- 69–Less = Needs to improve

A School-Site Improvement Standards Matrix can include a summary report of the 10 primary areas that have been evaluated by the key results team indicating the weighted score for each key indicator. The data can be presented in a bar chart format or in a similar table format to illustrate the variance in weighted average scores and to highlight the indicators that will require a schoolwide correction plan.

After the key results weighted scores have been tabulated, the school's principal and leadership team must identify specific indicators that require a corrective action plan. For example, a school that receives an 83% in lesson delivery will receive a grade of B. That same school, however, may also receive an overall score of 69% for student-centered environments. A score of 69% or below reflects a "need to improve." When a school receives a "needs to improve" rating, the school's principal and teacher-leaders must meet to create the school's corrective action plan. A corrective action plan that can improve a student-centered environment may consider the following strategies (Compton Unified School District School Operations, 2000):

1. Encouraging more cooperative learning in the classroom.

2. Displaying student work in the classroom.

3. Encouraging a teacher to use brainstorming and mind-mapping teaching strategies.

4. Using peers to provide continuous feedback.

5. Having students construct their own meanings with the curriculum presented.

6. Mentoring teachers to use cognitive tools with students.

CREATING VISIBILITY THROUGH FACILITY MANAGEMENT

School and district sites can leverage the support of their community members for the ongoing maintenance of existing facilities by creating visibility and accountability in facility management. Community partnerships can also provide support for school facility bond initiatives, which can fund the repair and development of new school facilities. School improvements from bonds and state initiatives include renovated auditoriums, new food facilities, bathroom remodels, fencing installations, roofing repairs, new doors and windows, installation of new heating and air conditioning units, Internet wiring and technology system upgrades, replacement of dilapidated bungalows, installation of security alarms, landscaping, playground equipment installations, and painting.

Campus safety and improved facilities contribute to a positive learning environment for students. The following strategies exemplify effective facility management strategies:

- Organizing facility inspections to ensure that all students in urban schools have access to safe, clean, and secure learning environments.
- Creating a Facility Grading Matrix that can be used at facilities' inspections to identify any concerns and to develop a corrective action plan that responds to specific concerns.
- Creating parent safety committees that will support the school's leadership in providing a clean, safe, and secure learning environment for students.

A facility master plan can help a school district focus its time on creating an environment conducive to student achievement. The plan can ensure that a school district provides students with a safe, clean, and secure school and can increase management effectiveness in a facility's daily operations and maintenance. The following steps can ensure a comprehensive master plan process (Fields Devereaux Architects & Engineers, 2001):

1. The evaluation team conducts an assessment of existing facilities, including architectural, structural, mechanical, electrical, and hazardous materials.

2. The team analyzes projected growth patterns and trends for the school district.

3. Based on the facility assessment and analyses, the evaluation team makes recommendations for upgrading school district facilities to meet safety, seismic, and handicap access codes. Upgrades can include school-site improvements, installing new mechanical systems, eliminating old and worn buildings, and building new schools to accommodate growth patterns.

4. The school master plan should be created with community member input and participation by forming a steering committee.

5. When engaging community members in the planning process, opportunities for community member access to school services should be enhanced, and schools should act as learning centers for their communities.

6. Data should be collected on the school capacity, enrollment projections, neighborhood density, and assets to assist in the district's creation of a master plan. A community's assets can include all other schools in the area, libraries, parks, health facilities, transit services, childcare agencies, community organizations, and businesses.

7. The steering committee should visit the district facilities to identify each school's needs and assets.

8. The steering committee should identify funding sources for school-based community services.

9. Schools should invite community members that stimulate creative and thought-provoking solutions to various school events and facility planning sessions.

In addition to creating a strategic facility master plan, the school can ensure the safety of all facilities while preserving the infrastructure of the school. The school's safety plan should include policies and procedures for using appropriate preparation techniques in response to a school-site fire, earthquake, or emergency drill. The school principal must (a) meet the standards of all building codes, (b) establish a systematic program of prevention maintenance, (c) regularly inspect all facilities and equipment, (d) promote energy efficiency, and (e) engender a sense of pride in the school's facility as part of an ongoing service-learning beautification project for the entire school community (Ramsey, 2001).

Schools can monitor and track facility needs and improvements by maintaining a criteria assessment for the physical plant and by tracking improvements on facility status reports. Form 2.1 includes a sample criteria assessment for the school's physical plant. Form 2.2 includes a sample facility status report. Once the physical plant criteria assessment is completed, the school can receive a grade based on its assessment and plan for improvement and repair.

Parent safety committees can be organized to monitor the school facility's safety and maintenance to ensure that all students have a safe, secure, and attractive place that facilitates their learning experiences. Parent safety committees can receive leadership training in the fall to help them develop the skills necessary for facility assessment and oversight. Once the parent safety committee chair and members are trained, the parents can be led through site visits to identify assets in the school, the adjacent neighborhoods, and to prioritize needs based on this research.

After analyzing assets and needs, the parent safety committee can define a project that they can develop at the school site. Project examples include (a) training parents and their children on safety procedures at the time of an emergency, (b) organizing first aid certification classes as a part of the training for parent volunteers who work at the schools, and (c) creating emergency kits of food, water, and gear for the school in case of an emergency. Parent safety committees can also be trained to seek funding for their various projects. Moreover, parents can encourage their children to participate

Form 2.1   Sample Physical Plant Criteria Assessment

Facility Criteria	Yes	No
The school site is safe, is free of fire hazards, has a safety plan, provides emergency access, and conducts ongoing drills per code. Comments:		
The school's classrooms and facility have windows that are operable, maintained, and clean. Comments:		
The school's restrooms are clean and have operable plumbing, windows, and fixtures. Comments:		
The school's cafeteria is clean and pleasantly appointed and has operable plumbing and appliances. Comments:		
The school's electrical, heating, and plumbing are adequate and hazards have been corrected and maintained. Comments:		

(Continued)

Form 2.1   (Continued)

Facility Criteria	Yes	No
The school's landscaping, playground equipment, and campus are clean and maintained with sufficient collection bins. Comments:		
The school's fences are properly installed, safe, and properly maintained. Comments:		
The roof is properly repaired and has adequate rain gutters and sufficient drainage. Comments:		
The technology equipment is installed with Internet connectivity and appropriate systems maintenance. Comments:		
The facility is freshly painted and has a graffiti abatement and maintenance plan. Comments:		
Other Comments:		

Form 2.2   Sample Facility Status Report

Location and Scope of Work	Date Request was Received	Proposed Start Date	Proposed Completion Date	Status/ Comments

in school- and community-based service-learning projects that promote health and safety services in the school community.

WORKING WITH LEGISLATORS

Building strong alliances and relationships with key legislators can help schools and the district leverage critical resources at times of crisis. These partnerships can also provide ongoing support for vital educational programs that respond to the unique learning needs of a low-performing school community. Relationships with legislators can meet the following school and district needs. They can:

- Assist schools and districts in overcoming hardships and in obtaining the resources required to sustain continued growth that responds to the changing demographics of a challenged and low-performing school community.
- Provide the essential support necessary for the implementation of innovative program reform initiatives that will increase student achievement and that can sustain the economic development of an urban school community.
- Utilize state-sponsored fiscal response services when a school or school district is challenged.
- Network and build effective public relations with other legislators to enhance both the school's and the district's ability to leverage support and resources for sustained and new program development to meet the diverse school community needs.

Although the federal government has never assumed a major role in education, its interest in education has been significant in setting a tone for the direction of education. Goals 2000, the federal school reform legislation, focuses on primary goals. These include school readiness, school completion, student achievement and citizenship, teacher education and development, student performance in mathematics and science, adult literacy and lifelong learning, safe schools, student discipline, alcohol- and drug-free schools, and parental participation in the school (Fiore, 2002).

Since the creation of the Goals 2000 legislation, state governments have been instrumental in creating educational state standards and funding legislation that support and reinforce these goals and the overall Goals 2000 theme that no child should be left behind. This groundbreaking federal legislation continues to have significant implications when considering the plight of low-performing schools.

In recent years, legislators have scrambled to fund initiatives that can support the needs of disenfranchised students. Urban, multistressed, and low-performing schools are using this legislation to create prescriptive programs that typically fall short in their performance outcomes. Many low-performing schools struggle with program implementation partly because of the overwhelming daily survival stresses imposed on the school's principal and teacher-leaders.

The current focus on a low-performing school's accountability is based on a marketlike view that schools should be managed like a business. The business view advocates that there should be financial rewards for performance, less funding for failures, and the role for government should be to improve student performance (Lester & Stewart, 2000). Political values, moral values, and social beliefs continue to plague legislators in how to best address the needs of the most economically challenged communities. There is a lack of agreement on what schools should teach students and how schools can best serve the diverse learning needs of their low-performing students (Spring, 2000).

RECEIVING SUPPORT FOR IMPLEMENTING PROGRAM REFORM INITIATIVES

The school district can serve as a major determining factor for the adoption, implementation, and institutionalization of program reform initiatives. The locus of policy making at the district level can sometimes deter effective reform at the school level. Supportive policy frameworks designed to act at the district level have the potential to support reform at the school level (Englert, 1993). The delicate balancing act of policy making and school reform program developments requires effective community relations that respond to the political nature of the school community (Sanders, 1999). Effective school-based strategies for increasing political resources require that the principal and teacher-leaders should do the following (Anderson, 1981; King & Stivers, 1998):

- Initially clarify the roles of all partners.
- Encourage the decision makers to vote with them.
- Determine why each decision maker should have an interest in their needs.
- Look for other collaborators and fully engage them in the process.
- Represent the needs of as many stakeholders from the school community as possible.
- Build a solid infrastructure in the school community to ensure successful reform efforts.
- Seek out timely support and cut deals as much as possible.
- Write to influence legislators and decision makers.
- Use a team approach.
- Role-play for consistency.
- Create success stories to support their cause.
- Ask for support.
- Agree on what they want to accomplish in a meeting before going into it and use their site for negotiations if at all possible.
- Be respectful while working through any negotiation.
- Create the strongest and most positive view of a position to influence change.

Low-performing school districts can work in partnership with the state in identifying a subcontractor who can assist the school in its assessment and recovery plan on a systematic basis. State-sponsored fiscal response services include tracking and identifying key school reform initiatives that support personnel management, pupil achievement, financial management, facilities management, and community relations. Once a state-sponsored fiscal response service completes an extensive audit of a school district's functions, a report can be generated on a predetermined schedule evaluating the school district's progress in correcting the various deficiencies. After a specific concern has received a passing score during an audit update, the school district no longer needs to track its progress on that standard.

A state-sponsored fiscal response team can help a low-performing school district comply and meet its recovery plans. In addition to a systematic, districtwide assessment and the development of the recovery plan, a state-sponsored fiscal response team must determine whether the school district continues to make substantial progress in each area of concern.

Low-performing schools must create specific activities with legislators to ensure ongoing communication and a general understanding on the critical needs for services. A community relations program should be created to build a diversified group of stakeholders at the district level who will network for the district to secure resources and build healthy community relations. Prospective partners can include business, civic, and institutional leaders who are committed to building the image of a healthy school district and securing resources for individual schools. The diversified group of stakeholders should create an extensive outreach program through media relations, direct mail, the district's cable station, and community forums. Family, school staff, and students must coordinate public relations efforts to increase cooperation and service delivery among key stakeholders. A database of key community contacts should be maintained full time for efficiency and accountability.

Effective strategies for engaging the support of legislators in key educational issues include:

- Educating the governor about the needs of a school district so he or she will sign specific assembly bills that will generate funding and resources.
- Engaging a state legislator to form a committee to meet the needs of a low-performing school district and encouraging the legislator to meet with the community about the school district's status in addressing key reform issues.
- Organizing school tours with key state legislators.
- Lobbying for extended school-year programs to intensify the learning available to low-performing students.
- Creating a community partnership newsletter highlighting partnership activities with various legislators as well as with other key stakeholders.
- Creating public relations materials that highlight a low-performing school district's successes in meeting the diverse needs of the community schools.
- Creating a series of press releases highlighting the many successes of a low-performing school district in initiating multiple school reform initiatives and securing resources for improving school facilities and school programs.
- Creating a series of community letters to parents and community members on the condition and health of the school district.
- Creating an aggressive teacher-recruitment program with signing bonuses for fully credentialed teachers and for teachers who can fill positions in math, science, and special education.

3

Creating a
Key Results
Accountability
Process

A key results accountability process for individual school sites focuses on (a) an individual teacher's lesson delivery; (b) the quality of lesson plans and how they align to the district and the state standards; (c) a student-centered environment that includes clearly articulated classroom/school expectations and discipline; (d) the availability of appropriate textbooks and supplementary materials; (e) the access to and use of a classroom reading area and school library; (f) writing assessments; (g) the use of student portfolios, student assessment folders, rubric-scored work, and student testing data for adapting curriculum to meet individualized needs; and (h) a safety net service delivery system that supports classroom instruction.

The following accountability strategies can enhance the key results process:

- Understanding how infallible indicators, an assessment analysis, and a schoolwide zero-tolerance policy of no drugs, drinking, or violence can increase student achievement.
- Identifying how key results responses can be integrated into corrective action plans with impact.
- Analyzing what specific lessons can be learned from visitation teams at individual school sites and how those lessons will have a direct impact on classroom instruction, teacher recruitment, staff development, and results-based teacher evaluation.

Form 3.1 highlights a sample completed key results instrument that can be utilized to increase student achievement. Results indicators can be measured by key results team members observing the classroom and school environment, identifying evidence of specific instructional materials and student participation of educational activities in a classroom, and observing a teacher's instructional strategies and the student responses to these strategies. Form 3.2 provides a template for a school principal and teacher-leaders to construct their own key results instrument based on their district and state academic standards and other identified priorities determined by regulatory organizations, the school district, and the school's leadership team. Key results indicators can also be developed on the school's business practices, including student attendance documentation, collection and use of student assessment data, special education data management of students with special needs, data collection of English language learners, health compliance form documentation, technology and information systems management, assessment of supplemental services, a textbook accountability survey, and facility maintenance.

Form 3.1   Sample Key Results Indicator Instrument

Directions: After each indicator, check whether or not you observe evidence of specific classroom materials, student behaviors, or instructional behaviors.

Classroom Number: *15*   School: *Achievement Elementary*

Grade Level: *1*   Job Classification of Observer: *Primary Grade Teacher*

Name of Teacher in   Number of Students: *20*
Attendance: *Mr. Stubbs*

Key Indicator	Evidence	No Evidence
Lesson delivery Students are responsive to the teacher's instructional strategies. The teacher is using multiple modality instructional strategies.	✓	
Classroom and school libraries The classroom has an age-appropriate library and instructional materials with a motivational reading program. The school library has a computer and age-appropriate software.		✓
Writing assessment The teacher has created a grade-level writing program and has posted the writing standards, and students are using the stages of writing process in different writing domains.	✓	
Lesson plans The lesson plan is available in the classroom and includes activities that reflect grade-level proficiency and evidence of lesson integration with connection to real-life experiences.	✓	

(Continued)

Form 3.1 (Continued)

Key Indicator	Evidence	No Evidence
Student-centered environment The classroom is organized and appealing, with student-generated class work on display and evidence of cooperative and project-based learning.		✓
Available instructional materials The classroom is equipped with core textbooks for each student and age-appropriate instructional and technological equipment.	✓	
Test preparation plan The teacher displays a test preparation implementation plan in the classroom with a student academic performance summary in the classroom's assessment binder.	✓	
Safety nets for students at risk of not meeting state standards The teacher adapts the reading and basic subjects curriculum to meet the developmental needs of at-risk students.	✓	
Safety nets for exceptional students (e.g., English language learner, gifted and talented, special education) The teacher has adjusted the reading and basic subjects curriculum to meet the individualized developmental needs of diverse students as evidenced by specific lesson plans for identified students.	✓	
Protection of instructional time in the classroom The teacher has the instructional implementation plan available in the classroom and there is evidence that attendance documentation and other nonessential instructional activities do not impose on the instructional day.	✓	

SOURCE: Compton Unified School District School Operations (2000).

Form 3.2   Key Results Indicator Template

Directions: After each indicator, check whether or not you observe evidence of specific classroom materials, student behaviors, or instructional behaviors.

Classroom Number: School:

Grade Level: Job Classification of Observer:

Name of Teacher in Attendance: Number of Students:

Key Indicator	*Evidence*	*No Evidence*
Lesson delivery		
Classroom and school libraries		
Writing assessment		
Lesson plans		
Student-centered environment		
Available instructional materials		
Test preparation plan		
Safety nets for students at risk of not meeting state standards		
Safety nets for exceptional students (e.g., English language learner, gifted and talented, special education)		
Protection of instructional time in the classroom		

SOURCE: Compton Unified School District School Operations (2000).

UNDERSTANDING HOW ASSESSMENT
INDICATORS CAN INCREASE STUDENT ACHIEVEMENT

Once a school's principal and leadership teachers create the various teacher and student academic performance indicators and benchmarks to be assessed by a key results team, student achievement can be tracked by individual classrooms. Typically, teachers who adapt the grade-level curriculum to meet the individualized needs of students report higher achievement gains as indicated in the high scores they receive in their key results indicators.

Teachers of students with special needs must have current individual education plans and psychoeducational reports on file for each student listed on a special needs class list. Effective teachers of special needs students meet with appropriate school personnel to understand how best to serve the unique learning needs of these students. Special needs students must receive supplemental services beyond the classroom on a predetermined schedule with demonstrated progress in meeting their individual goals and objectives. Teachers should confirm that special needs students have annual updates and reviews of their individual education plans. Teachers must also follow the school district policies and procedures for providing children with special education testing after receiving written permission from the parents within a predetermined response time.

Teachers of English language learners should review their students' English language survey and assessment information to determine the individual learning needs of all students. Teachers should verify that students have been properly placed in English development classes, including structured English immersion, sheltered English immersion, and English mainstream classes. In the English mainstream classes, classroom teachers should create small-group learning opportunities for students to practice their skill development and build confidence in learning. Curriculum should be adapted for real-life learning relevancy. Added services for special needs and at-risk students can include extra tutorial support services, an afterschool family literacy and career development program, mentoring programs, and career developing training in an afterschool sheltered work environment (Stanton-Salazar, 2001).

Integrating Key Results Into Corrective Action Plans

As school principals and teacher-leaders identify key results indicators that require improvement, the school's leadership team can create responsive corrective action plans. Figure 3.3 provides a sample self-assessment instrument with activities listed for corrective action in creating a classroom library and a student-centered environment.

Added library development activities may include:

- Creating a schoolwide library program that supports the development of classroom libraries in addition to a school's central library.
- Creating a rotational program where 60 books are rotated from the classroom to the school library every six weeks.
- Incorporating technological literacy in the library plan by developing multimedia standards for students.
- Creating a library technology master plan that includes purchasing computers and technology to support literacy development in each teacher's classroom.
- Creating a library family literacy program to share the resources with children and their families during extended weekday evening hours.
- Creating a literacy family training program to teach parents during the extended evening hours how to support their children's literacy development skills and to help parents learn how to help their children with their homework.

Figure 3.3   Sample School-Site Self-Assessment Corrective Action Plan

Directions: After each indicator, confirm or demonstrate evidence of specific classroom materials, student behaviors, or instructional behaviors.

Classroom Number: *15*   School: *Achievement Elementary*

Grade Level: *1*   Job Classification of Observer: *Primary Grade Teacher*

Name of Teacher in   Number of Students: *20*
Attendance: *Mr. Stubbs*

Key Indicator	Identify Weaknesses and List Specific Activities to Improve Student Achievement	Time
Lesson delivery		
Classroom and school libraries	The classroom does not have a library and there is no evidence of a reading motivation program.	9/0X
	Identify 60 age-appropriate paperback books for the classroom with the school district's classroom book fund.	10/0X
	Organize a Scholastic Book Club program to ensure bonus point collection for future book and magazine collections.	11/0X
	Contact the local newspapers to participate in the educational school reading incentive program. Create a book-reading area and an incentive program for students to complete book reports. Create a classroom poster to track completed books for each student with opportunities to win bonus points for extra classroom privileges.	10/0X
		10/0X
Writing assessment		

(Continued)

Figure 3.3   (Continued)

Key Indicator	Identify Weaknesses and List Specific Activities to Improve Student Achievement	Time
Lesson plans		
Student-centered environment	The classroom is not organized, lacks a student library, and does not have bulletin boards with student-generated work.	9/0X
	The library will be developed under the classroom library development program with access to books, magazines, and newspapers.	10/0X
	Create monthly bulletin board themes using student-generated work that has been graded using the grade-level writing assessment instrument.	9/0X & ongoing
	Organize parent volunteers to assist in monthly classroom bulletin board decorating and periodic classroom cleaning days.	10/0X & ongoing
Available instructional materials		
Test preparation plan		
Safety nets for at-risk students		
Safety nets for exceptional students		
Protection of instructional time		
Other:		
Other:		
Other:		

SOURCE: Compton Unified School District School Operations (2000).

- Creating a family story time program for parents to learn how to read to their children effectively and to create academic enrichment of activities to reinforce reading skills.
- Creating a schoolwide reading incentive program, including the principal providing the students with a party and a schoolwide enrichment day when all students read a total of 12 supplemental books a year.
- Creating a parent volunteer program to support the school's literacy development program and to help staff with extended library hours.

Added student-centered environment improvements can include (Burke & Picus, 2001):

- Creating small learning centers with desks for cooperative learning and project-based learning experiences.
- Creating a classroom-based technology center that provides students with computers, audiovisual equipment, and a digital camera that can record learning experiences.
- Partnering with businesses to create project-based, real-life work simulated learning experiences.
- Creating classroom-based science experimentation centers, social studies centers, and language learning centers.

Form 3.4 provides a template for a school's leadership team to create a corrective action plan. Action plans should be consistent with both the district and the school priorities to measure progress to date. Technical assistance from appropriate departments can be incorporated for each key indicator action plan. School leadership teams should also (a) monitor and report their progress of each action plan; (b) report student achievement with recommendations for continued improvement; (c) reassign staff and resources for action plan implementation; and (d) maintain budget constraints imposed by the district for fiscal accountability.

Form 3.4   School-Site Self-Assessment Corrective Action Plan
            Template

Directions: After each indicator, confirm or demonstrate evidence of specific classroom materials, student behaviors, or instructional behaviors.

Classroom Number: School:

Grade Level: Job Classification of Observer:

Name of Teacher in Attendance: Number of Students:

Key Indicator	Identify Weaknesses and List Specific Activities to Improve Student Achievement	Time
Lesson delivery		
Classroom and school libraries		
Writing assessment		
Lesson plans		
Student-centered environment		
Available instructional materials		

(Continued)

Form 3.4   (Continued)

Key Indicator	Identify Weaknesses and List Specific Activities to Improve Student Achievement	Time
Test preparation plan		
Safety nets for at-risk students		
Safety nets for exceptional students		
Protection of instructional time		
Other:		
Other:		
Other:		
Other:		

SOURCE: Compton Unified School District School Operations (2000).

Identifying School-Site Visitation Lessons

School-site visitations can help schools learn the following lessons:

1. Principals and teachers must focus on classroom instruction.

2. Principals must hire energetic, no-excuse teachers with high expectations.

3. Principals and district office administrators cannot fire everyone who has a history with the school's underperformance. The principal and district office administrators must focus on building capacity and hiring the right teachers and administrators to support the reform process.

4. Results are based on evaluations with rewards.

5. Principals should recognize the importance of a relationship-based culture.

6. Principals and district office administrators must frequently communicate with teachers and staff by using various communications channels.

7. Principals and teachers must stop the bleeding and losses generated from low-performing schools and focus on the checks and balances of each school's corrective action plan.

8. The principal must define achievement benchmarks and frequent assessments for meeting them.

9. Principals and district office administrators must limit promises and focus on accountability.

10. Principals and district office administrators must guard against choreographed chaos and distractions.

11. Principals and district office administrators must overmonitor students' academic progress.

12. Principals and district office administrators should highlight early successes to breed more successful growth.

13. The school site and district must focus on stable and consistent quality leadership.

14. Failure is not an option. It is only a nagging possibility that keeps principals and teacher-leaders focused.

4

Developing Trailblazing Initiatives That Guarantee Student Success

Trailblazing initiatives and reform strategies can serve as safety net services beyond the classroom for low-performing students in diverse low-performing school settings. Innovative initiatives can include creating aggressive teacher recruitment and development programs to attract talented, dedicated individuals who have completed college but who have not completed a teaching credential. After completing a rigorous selection process, teacher candidates must commit two years to teach in a low-performing school. The selected candidate will have the opportunity to complete their teaching credential while teaching and learning how to respond to the unique learning needs of diverse students. Added benefits for candidates can include receiving intensive school preparation, attending a full series of professional development activities on learning theories and teaching strategies, and receiving curriculum training aligned to the district and the state standards (Kritek, 1993).

Safety net programs that can boost student success include a reading recovery program that uses specially trained teachers to provide one-on-one reading instruction and evaluation to at-risk kindergarten through third-grade students. A corrective reading program designed for middle school students can provide individualized corrective reading interventions for academically challenged sixth-through ninth-grade students. Other tutorial programs can target homeless children and their families, preschool children enrolled in Head Start Programs and their families, and English language learners and their parents at the school site.

Reform programs that can increase student achievement include the following:

- Creating motivational attendance programs for students at individual school sites that acknowledge and reward students for prompt and regular school attendance.
- Organizing an accelerated learning program for underachieving students that includes an early primary learning program (full-day kindergarten classes), extended-day language development training, literacy instruction, numeracy training, tutorial services, a homework club, computer-assisted instruction, project-based learning, and service-learning opportunities in the community.
- Providing an extended school year for students that reinforces language arts, literacy, and numeracy skill development.
- Establishing a curriculum alignment backloading process that aligns curriculum to the content and con-text of standards-based mandated testing requirements.

CREATING MOTIVATIONAL
ATTENDANCE PROGRAMS

A motivational attendance program that acknowledges students for prompt and regular attendance is a school reform initiative that provides immediate results. Students with prompt and regular attendance tend to have better grades and are more likely to graduate (Reeves, 2000). Attendance incentive programs include:

- Recognizing students at school assemblies for perfect monthly attendance.
- Featuring students with perfect attendance in newsletter articles.
- Offering perfect attendance coupons for free books.
- Offering attendance privileges.
- Having students collect certificates for prompt and perfect attendance, which allow them to participate in raffles.
- Flying school attendance flags for reaching the school's attendance goals.
- Providing pizza and outside barbecue lunches on a monthly basis.
- Promoting recognition events at board meetings.
- Rewarding school budgets with discretionary funds for meeting yearly goals.

Teachers can also be encouraged to increase their attendance rates to 98% while student attendance rates can be targeted at 96%.

ORGANIZING AN ACCELERATED
LEARNING PROGRAM

Organizing an accelerated learning program can reduce student failure while eliminating social promotion. More low-performing schools are promoting and retaining students based on the attainment of basic skills, with an emphasis on reading, by using a variety of assessments. An accelerated learning program targeting low-performing youth can provide individualized academic attention in specifically targeted literacy areas. Typically, a program will track all students, kindergarten through eighth grade, at benchmark grade levels (e.g., in the third, fifth, and eighth grades) to identify students in danger of being retained. Parents will be notified during the first quarter that their child may be retained if the school's safety net programs do not sufficiently help the student increase his or her reading level within a year and a half of his or her present grade. Possible safety net services can include school-based tutoring programs staffed by extra duty credentialed teachers and private vendor tutorial programs managed at the school.

Continuous and regularly scheduled literacy assessments in November, February, and May provide valuable data to teachers on student instructional needs and can help identify the students in danger of retention. Students with low scores are then enrolled in a summer program for added support. Students retained at their previous grade level in September will be required to enroll in an accelerated learning program for intensive support to ensure that they will receive critical individualized instruction. Retained students will also receive vocabulary and numeracy training, homework club tutoring, a writer's workshop, computer-assisted instruction, project-based learning experiences, and community-based service-learning experiences. The goal for an accelerated learning program is to improve student reading abilities by more than 1.5 grade levels.

PROVIDING AN EXTENDED SCHOOL-YEAR PROGRAM

An extended school-year program adds to the number of days students attend school by having students attend during the summer months. The extended school-year program can be mandatory for students who are two or more grade levels behind in English, language arts, or mathematics. The determination that a student is performing two or more grade levels below his or her assigned class can be measured through standardized testing, assessments, proficiency tests for graduation, and district criterion-referenced tests based on the state standards. An initiative to extend the school year can be funded by governmental legislation created by the school district leaders.

The extended school-year program can focus on literacy development, math and science enrichment, visual and performing arts, health, and wellness education. Students can participate in field trips to local colleges, museums, science labs, hospitals, historical sites, and nature study sites. Teachers in the program can enhance their teaching skills by participating in staff development activities to increase their learning theories and teaching strategies. Professional development activities can include a summer institute on literacy and algebra, strategies for meeting the needs of diverse learners, and creating a schoolwide vision for literacy improvement.

BACKLOADING FOR CURRICULUM ALIGNMENT

The lesson plans that teachers use in classroom instruction must be aligned to the state's content standards, the district's curriculum guide, and the state's mandated assessments for a specific grade level. By backloading the curriculum to meet state-mandated testing requirements and content standards, teachers become more responsive to individual student needs and adapt the curriculum to address deficiencies in prior learning experiences. Backloading assures 100% alignment to the test because the test is used as the basis for defining what is to be aligned (Curriculum Management Audit Centers, 2000).

This survival strategy is commonly used by low-performing schools and continues to be criticized by test manufacturers and state departments of education. Test makers typically measure for skill attainment by using a normal curve frequency distribution (i.e., a bell curve) designed to assess the results of larger populations with the assumption that all students in a given grade level start with the same level of subject proficiency (English, 1992). The assumption is that there is no need to consider the social or economic class, the cultural capital, or the selected cultural content and linguistic patterns of specific groups of students attending a school (Curriculum Management Audit Centers, 2000; English, 1992).

Another backloading disadvantage is that some teachers have trouble discerning how to teach to the test, and a faulty teaching strategy can skew the curriculum out of proportion in certain subject areas (Curriculum Management Audit Centers, 2000).

After the curriculum at a specific grade level is defined and aligned to state and national standards, a grid can be developed showing the unit activities on the left side of the lesson plan and how these unit activities tie to the standards and testing objectives on the right side of the lesson plan (Comer, Ben-Avie, Haynes, & Joyner, 1999). Teachers can also analyze the results of a specific class's performance on a standardized test and link the teacher's workplan to the deficiencies identified in the testing data. Pacing charts and curriculum maps can be created that emphasize areas where student performance is poor and where concentrated teaching must occur (English, 1992). Deep curriculum alignment ensures that teachers become familiar with the content and the context of the state's mandated assessment for students and that students can transfer the curriculum content learned in the classroom to the correct standardized test responses (Curriculum Management Audit Centers, 2000).

Students can also receive achievement reports that identify grade-level standards and the level of proficiency that a student has attained on a specific date, the teacher's comments about a student's needs, a plan for corrective action for meeting specific standards, and a parent's comments in responding to the proposed plan (Reeves, 2000). Additionally, teachers can take a classroom assignment and break it into standards-based learning units. Individual students can be assessed at their level of proficiency for each unit measured. A further analysis can include specific benchmark dates that indicate when a student achieves each benchmarked unit, the frequency that a student applies a new concept or skill within a specific project, and a portfolio assessment analysis completed by the student and the teacher measuring the process the student used to achieve a specific standard (Burke, Baca, Picus, and Jones, 2003).

Challenges to these various levels of assessments and backloading strategies can include (a) the principal's and teacher's ability to efficiently collect and analyze data at regular intervals to address individual classroom needs; (b) the district staff's ability to provide schools with the staff development training and testing collection support necessary to conduct these curriculum and instruction audits; and (c) the school principal's and teachers' ability to effectively track a teacher's performance and student's performance over time. Each year, students are reassigned to different teachers and teachers receive a new combination of students. Different combinations of students create different classroom learning environments. Teachers' levels of teaching effectiveness can vary with individual groups of students, and an individual student's performance can vary with different teachers and combinations of students. The dynamics of classroom teaching and learning must be considered when conducting curriculum and instruction audits on any one group of students or on a teacher's classroom environment over time.

Form 4.1 provides an example of a backloaded first-grade mathematics curriculum lesson. Form 4.2 provides a lesson plan with academic standards that a teacher can use for backloading curricular activities.

Form 4.1   Sample Backloaded Curriculum Lesson Plan

First-Grade Mathematics Unit Objectives	First-Grade Mathematics Standards and Testing Objectives
1.1 Students will write the number of various object patterns in their math book up to 100. 1.2 Students will demonstrate their ability to read math problems using numbers up to 100. 1.3 Students can count to 100 as demonstrated in various number songs	1.1 Students can count, read, and write whole numbers to 100.
2.1 Students can demonstrate their ability to add by counting the pencils in a pack of 10 pencils and adding pencils from another pack of pencils to count a total of 20 pencils. 2.2 Students can demonstrate their ability to subtract by counting the pencils in a pack of 20 pencils and subtracting each pencil as they distribute the pencils to 15 classmates to retain a balance of 5 pencils in the pack.	2.1 Students can show the meaning of addition and subtraction.
3.1 Students can sort collections of buttons by color or shape and count the correct number of each sorted group 3.2 Students can create number patterns by organizing specific colors of buttons in a pattern of first one red button, then two white buttons, and then another red button. This number pattern can be repeated until a total of thirty buttons have been sorted and placed in a pattern.	3.1 Students can sort objects and create and describe number shapes, sizes, and number patterns.

SOURCE: Curriculum Development and Supplemental Materials Commission, 2000.

Form 4.2   Blank Lesson Plan for Use in Backloading
a Curriculum

Directions: List the first-grade mathematics unit objectives your
school will use to meet the following first-grade standards and
testing objectives.

First-Grade Mathematics Unit Objectives	*First-Grade Mathematics Standards and Testing Objectives*
1.1 1.2 1.3	1.1 Students can count, read, and write whole numbers to 100.
2.1 2.2 2.3	2.1 Students can show the meaning of addition and subtraction.
3.1 3.2 3.3	3.1 Students can sort objects, create and describe number shapes, sizes, and number patterns.

SOURCE: Curriculum Development and Supplemental Materials
Commission, 2000.

Expanding Parent and Community Involvement Activities

Effective parent and community involvement activities provide schools and the district with the support required to overcome low-performing school challenges. Community participation keeps the lines of communication open between the school and community. Open communication should be responsive to ongoing community member concerns regarding the education of their students (Aronson, 1995). As parents and community members become more involved in schools, principals may struggle with how to best use the resources they provide to meet the diverse needs of their students.

The Search Institute has identified 40 crucial assets that students need to reach their full potential and to avoid at-risk behaviors. These assets include family support, caring neighborhoods, adult role models, a sense of purpose, and optimism about the future (Ramsey, 20001). Schools can support the development of these assets by engaging parents and community members to serve as volunteers in the schools. Effective volunteer development programs (a) define how a school can become a welcoming place for volunteers; (b) identify diverse stakeholders; (c) create a public relations plan with policies and procedures that support school and community partnerships; (d) train teachers and staff on how to support volunteer activities that focus on academic development; and (e) create community collaborations for ongoing resource and program development (Burke & Picus, 2001).

Examples of parent and community member involvement activities that can ensure the healthy development of schools include:

- Developing responsive parent committees that provide critical feedback on school and district policies, curricular modifications, school- and districtwide safety issues, academic safety net service delivery, and the development of new or expanded programs that respond to the individualized learning needs of the school community.
- Organizing regularly scheduled community forums with diverse stakeholder groups to provide potential partners with an update of the school and the district educational progress and to receive information and feedback on critical community issues that can affect the school's and district's delivery of services.
- Mobilizing community partners to support various reform initiatives, program development needs, and school beautification projects, and to leverage resources for a streamlined delivery of educational, health, and human care services.

DEVELOPING RESPONSIVE PARENT COMMITTEES FOR CRITICAL FEEDBACK

In addition to helping their child with homework and volunteering in their child's classroom, parents can be encouraged to participate in parent committees to provide critical feedback at their child's school. Parents can be trained on grade level skill development, curricular content that supports this skill development, and effective strategies for supporting students in their learning (Sanders, 1999). Parents can, for example, learn how to ask reading comprehension questions and guide students in learning how to further research a reading assignment by using the Internet and library resources.

Parents can also become active in developing school-based programs that are responsive to student academic needs and healthy development. They can provide critical program design and evaluation support. In afterschool childcare programs, parents can support the school's principal and teacher-leaders with feedback on how the program is responding to the childcare needs of the family and on the academic and social development of their children. Parents can also be encouraged to participate in schoolwide curricular information nights.

Reforming schools can create the following services to better support parents:

- Ongoing English language development classes provided at the school site
- Weekly evening family literacy nights
- Translations and interpretation services provided at all meetings and for all home and school correspondence
- A bilingual community worker to help parents communicate with the school's staff and various community agencies
- Phones in every classroom with voice mail and homework information
- A volunteer school program with parent training and recruitment for volunteering at the schools as translators or classroom helpers, for offering home support, and for helping with school beautification projects
- Quarterly parent-teacher conferences and standards based progress reports with translation services for English language learners

- A room parent program
- Parent education and academic support training and workshops
- A parent hotline

Principals should be encouraged to develop strong ties to the community. Because the key results recovery process specifically targets depressed and traditionally underserved communities, reforming schools should function as community hubs that can support the overall economic needs of the neighboring community (Oakes, Quartz, Ryan, & Lipton, 2000). Strong partnerships with the residents and businesses in the schools can be developed by:

- Creating a business and community mentorship program.
- Organizing school–business partnership adoptions.
- Developing extensive room parent programs.
- Creating an extensive public relations campaign.

Principals should forge business and social service partnerships that provide families with access to individual and family mental health counseling, healthcare, vision screening, and dental care. Businesses can provide teachers and students with skill development training in computers and technology.

ORGANIZING COMMUNITY FORUMS WITH DIVERSE STAKEHOLDERS

Community forums can be organized by the school district in partnership with the district schools. The purpose of community forums can be to meet and interact with the school community to identify concerns, problem solve, and discuss the overall short- and long-term goals of a school district in support of the various district schools. Community forums can also develop breakout sessions for problem solving.

Examples of community forum breakout topics include the following:

- A discussion on the school district mission and how it aligns to core values
- A description of the district's accountability plan and its overall support of schools in achieving specific goals and objectives for increased student achievement
- An update on facility improvements and maintenance issues to assure community members that the school district is supporting schools in creating a safe and secure learning environment
- An update on school safety programs to reduce the incidence of crime on and around the school campus
- A discussion on textbook adoptions and how the curriculum supports the district's overall goals for student achievement
- A description of safety net services available to students requiring added academic support beyond the traditional program
- An overview of the various supplemental health, human care, and academic support programs available to students' parents and community members
- A summary of resource development strategies and an update on new grants, donations, and sponsorships the school district and individual schools have received to expand their educational services for students and their families
- A review of the various reform initiatives that the school district has implemented at the various school sites
- Other pertinent concerns and emerging programs that can be of interest to the greater school community

In addition to large community forums, school district superintendents, in partnership with school principals, can provide parents and community members with the current state-of-the-district and school-site reports. These reports can be scheduled quarterly, semiannually, or annually and highlight the various successes and challenges that the district and schools have achieved. Topics can focus on facilities and safety issues, educational improvements, staff hiring and development, and community outreach and partnership activities. After a brief presentation summarizing the school and district achievements, parents and community members can break into small groups to brainstorm solutions that address challenges.

For example, if a school is struggling to make its campus safer, the parents and community members may choose to increase the level of surveillance with community police and community watch groups. A special phone number can be created for anonymously reporting school break-ins, loitering, vandalism, and other suspicious activities. Financial rewards can be offered for any information leading to the arrest and conviction of persons who have destroyed or vandalized school property. Random searches with metal detectors can deter students from bringing weapons on campus. School and district staff can identify students who are cooperating with the school safety and security program and acknowledge their commitment for a safe and secure campus at student assemblies.

Parents can also participate in focus groups to assess parent and community involvement and can provide feedback to the school principal and teacher-leaders about their level of involvement and experiences with the school. Parents can be questioned on how the school can increase parent participation at the school site and can comment on a school's climate, communications, outreach efforts, the overall use of parent volunteers in the classroom, and parent volunteer support of the overall administration of the school. Parent volunteers can also canvass residential neighborhoods adjacent to the school wearing apparel indicating that they are school district volunteers or wearing official school district volunteer badges when approaching neighbors. The neighborhood visits can help the school principal and teacher-leaders learn more about parental lack of involvement at the school site. Parents and community members can also receive information about the school during the home visits to increase their participation.

Mobilizing Community Partners to Support Reform Initiatives

Parents and community volunteers can be mobilized to support school reform initiatives by becoming actively involved in learning more about the school and sharing their knowledge with the greater school community. Principals and teacher-leaders can create and disseminate progress reports about the school improvements on their key results indicators. School-site progress reports can include the following types of information:

- The number of newly hired teachers and staff
- The number and types of newly purchased textbooks and other curricular materials for a specific grade level
- A description of the new types of programs or services provided by the school
- The development of new safety net services to ensure that students are able to perform at their highest levels
- Effective class-size reduction strategies
- Strategies in making schools safer and more attractive
- New facility constructions and remodels
- Levels and types of parent and community involvement
- Strategies for adequately supporting students' diverse learning needs
- The student overall achievement tracked by grade-level data

School- and district-level advisory groups provide structures for obtaining information from all stakeholder groups. The school district and school sites can create community task force groups to study school reform issues such as student promotion and retention, transportation, facility development, adapting curriculum to meet the needs of English language learners, and engaging parents in the day-to-day learning of their children.

The community clergies can become advocates for raising student academic standards by educating parents about the value of education. On a designated Sunday, local church leaders can educate parents about their responsibility to educate their children through a special sermon. School volunteers in partnership with outstanding graduates or student leaders can share with congregations how their parents' commitment and involvement has made a difference in their academic performance and career development. Information about the school district and strategies for parent support in their children's learning can be circulated in the church. The religious leader can also provide a discussion on how to overcome obstacles for parent involvement (e.g., lack of time, language barriers, and lack of understanding the American school system). Local clergy can become part of a clergy advisory team with the school district to continue to provide input on community concerns and to learn more about the accomplishments of the school community.

The school community can sponsor ongoing health fairs with free health screenings, immunizations, nutritional data, and safety information for the families of students and community members. Health screenings can include blood pressure checks, vision and hearing screenings, dental checkups, and weight control evaluations. Health fairs can be coordinated with local hospitals, doctors, mental health professionals, public health nurses, and local health education agencies. Safety and career booths can be operated by the local police and fire departments.

As the school and district engage parents and community members to participate at their neighborhood school, the district can develop a volunteer information and enrollment packet. The volunteer packet can contain the district's mission statement for developing school-based volunteer services.

The following informational pieces should be part of the packet (Compton Unified School District, 1999):

- A personal information application form
- A request for documentation and clearance results of a TB skin test and/or X-ray
- Information on volunteer photo badges
- Information on volunteer orientation meetings
- A request for a fingerprint report from the state
- Volunteer participation guidelines and school-site packet of information, and a form to verify that these have been reviewed by the volunteer
- A volunteer job description and a form to verify that it has been reviewed by the volunteer
- A "promise to serve" form that specifies duration of time each week that a volunteer promises to give the school

Epstein, Coates, Salinas, Sanders, and Simon (1997) postulate that there are six types of parent and community involvement in schools:

Type 1 is designed to provide families with training in how to establish a supportive home environment for student learning through home visits, information on child-rearing practices, and family support programs.

Type 2 is a communication level of involvement with parent-teacher conferences, classroom newsletters, and weekly communication envelopes of students' work.

Type 3 represents the volunteering level of involvement and includes volunteer recruitment, training, participation in the classroom, and schoolwide administrative support.

Type 4 provides learning-at-home activities with a focus on the skills required for student success and how parents can support their children in their academic achievement.

Type 5 is the decision-making level of involvement with volunteers participating in the school's program development and overall administration. Volunteers can be actively involved in the school council, the school's parent-teacher-student activities organization, and district advisory committees on curricular and facility development.

Type 6 involvement activities include creating partnerships with various stakeholders to integrate community resources into a school's daily programs and to support the school's overall administration and management of resources.

Parents can serve as useful resources to help school principals and teacher-leaders implement school reform initiatives. Parents can be instrumental in helping school leaders accomplish the following activities:

- Parents can help teachers understand the needs of newcomers to the school community by providing teachers with information about different community services and resources for newly immigrated families and for families who recently relocated to the area.
- Parents can help teachers increase their understanding of student needs through parent-teacher conferences and through participation in various school advisory councils.
- Parents can provide cultural enrichment and performing arts activities through cultural school-based celebrations, cultural fairs, and academic enrichment activities.
- Parents can help schools build libraries, obtain classroom supplies, and organize school beautification and service-learning activities in the community.
- Parents can provide other parents with training on how to help in a classroom-based volunteer program and how to academically support their children's learning.
- Parents can tutor limited-English-speaking parent volunteers in basic subjects and provide training in how to access educational services for their children and their own professional growth.
- Parents can create afterschool and evening family literacy programs that will help students and their families

increase their language arts, mathematics, and computer literacy abilities.

- Parents can organize curricular make-and-take workshops where teachers educate parents on grade-level curriculum and instruct them in how to design reading and mathematics games and activities that can reinforce the classroom activities.
- Parents can organize and manage a parent center that includes training in the American school system, English-as-a-second-language (ESL) training, job interviews, and career development training. The center can house social services and basic-needs support services for low-income families. A mobile health clinic can come to the center weekly for immunizations and basic healthcare examinations.
- Parents can support the school in advocating for improved academic facilities through school bonds and other community organizing activities to leverage added resources.

Services that community organizations typically provide low-performing schools include counseling and case management services; food banks for low-income families; clothing exchange services for school uniforms; clothing for parents to attend school functions; eyeglasses for students; family literacy programs; book donations for school and family libraries; Internet connections for research; mentors; service-learning experiences; job-shadowing opportunities; and community revitalization projects for students and their families.

Once the parent or community member becomes an active volunteer in the school, it is critical that the volunteer submit a monthly volunteer log to the volunteer development office. Forms 5.1 and 5.2 provide sample parent and community volunteer tracking instruments that can be used for documenting the level of parent and community involvement in the schools using Epstein's (2001) levels of parent and community involvement.

Form 5.1 Sample Tracking Form for Identifying the Number of Parents and Community Volunteers Participating at Each Grade Level Using Epstein's Framework for Six Types of Parent Involvement

Directions: Identify the unduplicated number of parents and community volunteers at each grade level who have participated in the school using Epstein's framework for six types of parent involvement. If a parent has participated at the school at various levels of involvement or a various grade levels, count the parent's involvement at the highest level of involvement and/or at the highest grade level.

Grade Level	Type 1 Parent Education Support	Type 2 Conferences, Translation, and Phone Calls	Type 3 Recruiting for Volunteer Support	Type 4 Providing Academic Information for Home Support	Type 5 Recruiting for PTA and Advisory Groups	Type 6 Providing Community Resources and Building Partners

Form 5.2   Sample Tracking Form for Number of Times Parents and Community Volunteers Participate in School Activities at Each Grade Level Using Epstein's Framework for Six Types of Parent Involvement

Directions: Identify the frequency and or duplicated number of times parents and community volunteers at each grade level have participated at the school using Epstein's framework for six types of parent involvement.

Grade Level	Type 1 Parent Education Support	Type 2 Conferences, Translation, and Phone Calls	Type 3 Recruiting for Volunteer Support	Type 4 Providing Academic Information for Home Support	Type 5 Recruiting for PTA and Advisory Groups	Type 6 Providing Community Resources and Building Partners

6

Enforcing Effective Business Practices

By enforcing effective business practices, low-performing schools and districts can leverage resources to adequately serve the unique learning needs of individual students. Effective district office practices include internal audit activities that (a) evaluate the district's management of financial resources for schools, (b) reduce the number of reportable external audit findings, and (c) create adequate internal controls. Effective district offices create a curable year-end audit process with predetermined closing cycles that allow adequate time to enter all financial transactions into the financial database system.

Internal audit functions track student attendance, purchasing and contracting procedures, overtime expenditures, payroll accountability, grant compliance reporting requirements, asset and instructional materials inventory, loss management, and a host of other internal control challenges. Fiscal management recommendations with action plans and status reports can be highlighted. A contract management committee can assist school districts to identify and implement financial management standards that must be addressed through a quarterly evaluation and rating system.

Low-performing schools are not immune to excessive spending and therefore should practice a prudent spending policy by participating in an aggressive budget-monitoring process. Utility bills, workers' compensation claims, insurance costs, overtime, school-site vandalism, and textbooks are examples of costs that can become exorbitant without prudent monitoring. Utility bills can be decreased by having staff and students participate in an energy conservation program that includes (a) limiting the heating and air-conditioning temperature levels during the school day; (b) turning off electronic equipment and computers at night; (c) monitoring the usage of lights in classrooms and traffic areas to ensure safety and security; and (d) adjusting the school hours of operation and extended breaks to conserve utility usage. Additional costs can be saved by targeting students and their parents with a public relations campaign on textbook and library book return policies. Such a campaign can ensure that thousands of books are returned to the school at the end of each school year.

Workers' compensation claims can be reduced by conducting a claims audit that analyzes losses, handling procedures, and vendor utilization. Creating school-site safety committees with employee safety training and prevention incentives can further reduce workers' compensation losses. A school-site health and safety facility grading system can educate school stakeholders on the various health and safety issues on which a school site must improve for the overall health and safety of the school's students and staff. School district staff can monitor insurance costs by conducting an annual comparative analysis of various insurance carriers, the carrier's limits of coverage, and the carrier's claims settlement services.

School vandalism can be deterred by creating a school-site monitoring program that (a) designates a school-site employee to inspect the school building and the school site for any vandalism or graffiti each day; (b) has an internal reporting and monitoring process to facilitate school building and site repairs; and (c) has a vandalism grading system that can educate the school community on various vandalism concerns and on how the school staff is addressing ongoing facility and site vandalism maintenance. A school principal and teacher-leaders can also organize a school-based beautification program that encourages parent volunteers and students to beautify the school site monthly. School-based beautification activities can include painting, repairs, planting trees and flowers, weeding, cleaning, repairing playground equipment, and maintaining the overall beauty of the school grounds.

Student and staff attendance can significantly increase student achievement and school revenue each year. Tracking a school's attendance requires careful monitoring of attendance and absenteeism rates on a daily, weekly, and monthly basis. Parents must be consistently informed about the importance of student attendance through ongoing communications mailed from the school to the home. It is critical that parents also receive informational phone calls from a classroom teacher or from the school community liaison on days that their child is absent or tardy. Parents must be educated that children's school attendance is critical for academic success and that a school receives its funding from the state based on actual daily attendance (e.g., the actual number of students sitting in their seats at school each day). District office attendance tracking for each school can focus on the number of home visits provided by school community liaisons to student homes with excessive absences and the number of students who must be referred to a school district's discipline board for extended absences.

A school staff must become educated on the negative impact to the school mission, operations, and budget due to staff absences. Students require qualified teachers and support staff each day to facilitate optimal learning. Ongoing absences can negatively affect a student's ability to learn due to a lack of continuity of curricular content and limited support from aides and office staff. Substitute teachers must be hired in classrooms with absent teachers. Substitute teachers frequently lack adequate teaching credentials and experience to sufficiently support diverse student learners. This problem is accentuated at low-performing schools where large numbers of English language learners and students from economically challenged families are required to receive differentiated instruction in overcrowded and understaffed schools. Disciplinary procedures for dealing with staff attendance problems must be implemented in a methodical and consistent manner.

Low-performing schools typically have high turnover rates and require ongoing reassignment of teachers and administrators to compensate for a higher-than-average turnover rate. It is not uncommon for some low-performing schools to experience a 30% teacher turnover rate each year. Cost-effective staffing formulas can maximize the use of appropriate staffing in the areas of greatest need within a district and at various school sites. Staffing formulas include an evaluation of alternative expenditure strategies according to their cost-effectiveness in producing a specific outcome (Levin & McEwan, 2001). Table 6.1 illustrates a sample staffing allocation formula for various grade levels at a low-performing school district that receives extensive federal and state funding to support school improvement initiatives.

Securing Resources for School Sites

Strategies that can increase the success of securing aid from diverse funders include forming partnerships with parents, community-based organizations, governmental entities, businesses, universities, and cultural communities (Burke, 1999). Building effective partnerships with community groups and businesses can maximize and streamline both a district and school delivery of safety net, healthcare, and human care services. School principals and teacher-leaders can learn about available resources by creating a community portrait on the geographical location surrounding the school, the student home neighborhoods, and other locations the school families and teachers spend time at, including museums, zoos,

Table 6.1   Sample Staffing Allocation Formula

Position	Elementary	Middle	High
Principal	1	1	1
Vice principal	1	2	3
Teacher	Grades K–3 = 1/20 students Grades 4–5 = 1/32 students	Grades 6–8 = 1/32 students	Grades 9–12 = 1/32 students
Counselor	1	1/500 students	1/500 students
Secretary	1	1	1
Clerk typist	1	1	3
School community liaison	1	1	1
Librarian	0	0	1
Library aide	1	1	0
Classroom teaching aides	0	0	0

libraries, shops, childcare centers, and places of worship (Epstein, 2001).

Low-performing schools must partner with various governmental entities to build cities that can adequately support schools. Schools can have a generative and developmental impact on their surrounding urban communities (Parker, 1993). With the rise of the information technology and global economic competition, schools have focused their curricular offerings on increased science, math, and technology skills to support a technology-based economy. In recent years, big-city mayors have sought to increase their leverage over educational reform by supporting various bond issues and making educational initiatives central to their overall community commitment (Blakely, 1997). For example, schools can be viewed as asset-based community indicators, magnets for neighborhood disarmament, centers of community pride, facilitators for service learning and self-growth, or places for training about American democracy (Kerchner, 1997). Low-performing school principals and teacher-leaders must consider how school reform initiatives can influence a city official's understanding of schools.

Low-performing schools can be viewed as basic industries that will impact a community's overall development and economy. Historically, businesses have used schools to prepare workers for the workplace. School-business partnerships can affect the number of scientists and engineers preparing for careers as well as lower-skilled manual laborers (Spring, 2000). Currently, university schools of education are over-enrolling students to become teachers because of the projected shortage of teachers and educational administrators in the next decade.

Business partnership strategies include the following (Comer, Ben-Avie, Haynes, & Joyner, 1999):

- Businesses providing student apprenticeships for structured on-the-job training that supports school-to-work initiatives and includes workplace mentoring, job shadowing, and instruction in workplace competencies.
- Business leaders visiting students in classrooms to incorporate job-related skills that meet the district's and state's academic standards.
- Business leaders using students to support beta test site projects in a classroom for new product introduction and modification.
- Business leaders providing students with funding for college scholarships.
- Businesses sponsoring community field trips and equipment donations for schools.
- Businesses providing students with guest speakers on industry-related topics for career development.

- Business leaders using students to assist in the creation of products and to participate in marketing focus groups to evaluate new product development.
- Businesses providing teachers with industry-related staff development and internship programs.

Schools can join forces with universities to conduct community-based research and to develop new programs and products as a result of this research (Burke, 2002). For example, an AmeriCorps literacy project may produce a training program for new teachers of English language learners. A Healthy Start state-funded initiative may create training materials on how a school can conduct a needs assessment for the school and community to identify and prioritize critical basic health and welfare needs for students to be ready and adequately prepared to learn. Some universities form a governance management team with teachers, administrators, health professionals, and parents. This team manages a school's academics, social activities, and special projects to foster student psychological, social, and academic development.

Community cultural resources can help a school's principal and teacher-leaders promote the goals of the dominant culture (Parker, 1993). By becoming culturally proficient, low-performing schools are creating policies and practices that support the values and behaviors of students and the school stakeholders who reside in a culturally diverse community (Lindsey, Robins, & Terrell, 1999). Strategies for supporting cultural proficiency within a school include:

- Providing ongoing staff development for teachers on valuing diversity, assessing cultural values, managing differences, institutionalizing cultural knowledge, and adapting to diversity.
- Providing institutional support to students with cross-cultural and social resources that build on a student's home and community experiences.

- Promoting bilingualism, biculturalism, and binationalism.
- Providing students with additive caring and cultural sensitivity that build on students' bicultural experiences in their neighborhoods.

Ideally, the school principal and teacher-leaders must build off all stakeholder partnerships to improve the overall academic performance of their diverse student population. This collaboration can be viewed as the shared creation of diverse stakeholders with complementary skills that respond to the needs of a school (Fullan, 1993). Table 6.2 provides a sample workplan that a school's principal and teacher-leaders used to identify resources that they can obtain from various stakeholder groups for a school-based cultural community fair. Form 6.1 provides a workplan that school principals and teacher-leaders can use to identify the types of resources they can obtain from each stakeholder partner.

Table 6.2   Sample Workplan Identifying Resources for a School-Based Cultural Community Fair

Stakeholder Classification	Description of Resources
Parents	Parent volunteers will organize a cultural fair at the school site and create fundraising activities to support the event.
Community-based organizations	Ethnic community agencies will provide informational brochures about their various services. The Mexican Community Agency and the Asian American Agency will provide ethnic dancers for the event. Various ethnic agencies will provide culturally sensitive food booths at the event for fundraising.

(Continued)

Table 6.2   (Continued)

Stakeholder Classification	Description of Resources
Governmental entities	The City of Care will provide a mini event-planning grant to fund food and entertainment. The Diversity County will provide a mini grant for translation services at the event for monolingual participants.
Businesses	Gonzales Party Supplies will donate piñatas and candy for the event's entertainment. Lee Stationers will provide Chinese New Year coin packets. Aztec Folklore will donate Native American art and jewelry for event prizes.
Universities	The American College will donate language majors to provide translation services for event participants. The United College will donate program evaluators to determine what impact the event will have on participants.
Cultural communities	The Taos Pueblo Indians will teach school-aged children how to dance various tribal ceremonial dances. Immigrants from Mexico will organize cultural diversity and sensitivity classes for school-aged children. Vietnamese immigrants will create a Vietnamese banquet for event participants and provide cooking demonstrations at the event.

Form 6.1   Securing Resources Workplan Using Diverse
Stakeholders

Stakeholder Classification	Description of Resources
Parents	
Community-based organizations	
Governmental entities	
Businesses	
Universities	
Cultural communities	
Other:	
Other:	
Other:	

Identifying and Seeking
Alternative Program Funding Solutions

School budgets are never sufficient. All stakeholder groups must become involved in resource development to ensure that schools leverage ample supplies, equipment, and financial support to accommodate their extensive needs. Linkages between stakeholders can include networking, coordination, cooperation, collaborative resource utilization, and a plan involving the total community (Ramsey, 2001). Community partners can collaborate in a school's service delivery by bringing existing resources to the school site and modifying these services to better meet the needs of its student population.

At the beginning of each school year, the school principal and leadership teachers should organize a staff retreat to (a) identify various programs and classroom resources that individual teachers and the school need in order to meet the performance objectives for the year; (b) create and distribute a strategic planning assessment instrument to identify and prioritize various classroom and school needs; (c) identify prospective funders for prioritized needs; and (d) create an action plan for seeking alternative funding sources. A schoolwide assessment process can also include an analysis of the school's plan for student achievement, an examination of the overall grade-level and school achievement data, an evaluation of students' work in relation to the state standards and testing results, and an evaluation of the curricular content and teaching strategies provided to students at various grade levels. Form 6.2 provides a sample planning assessment instrument to help identify and prioritize a school's needs. Form 6.3 provides a sample prospective funder worksheet.

Form 6.2   Sample Planning Assessment for Identifying and Prioritizing Needs

Directions: Consider the following schoolwide program and teacher classroom needs for your school. Circle the appropriate numerical value (1 = *low* and 5 = *high*) to rate the priority for obtaining resources or funding for this need.

	Low				*High*
1. The teacher's classroom has sufficient textbooks.	1	2	3	4	5
2. The teacher has sufficient curricular training and teaching strategies to support diverse student needs.	1	2	3	4	5
3. The teacher utilizes a writing rubric in a schoolwide writing program.	1	2	3	4	5
4. The teacher's classroom is student-centered with an organized arrangement of desks and teaching materials. Bulletin boards display current student work reinforcing key teaching strategies.	1	2	3	4	5
5. The teacher's classroom has adequate instructional materials and audiovisual and technology equipment to support student learning and academic achievement.	1	2	3	4	5
6. The classroom teacher uses school-level and classroom academic achievement data along with diverse teaching strategies to support students in their learning.	1	2	3	4	5
7. The teacher's classroom and teaching strategies are organized to maximize the use of instructional time dedicated to student academic achievement.	1	2	3	4	5
8. The teacher understands how to provide individual students with safety net services to prevent low performance, and the teacher is aware of the various safety net services available to students at the school site and through district office services.	1	2	3	4	5
9. The school library is sufficiently stocked with a wide range of grade-level books that will support students' diverse needs.	1	2	3	4	5
10. The school has developed a comprehensive language arts program that reflects the district and state standards and that features trained teachers who understand how to integrate reading, language arts, and writing curriculum into their daily plans.	1	2	3	4	5
11. The school environment is student-centered with organized classrooms and plant layout. Bulletin boards display current student work reinforcing key teaching strategies.	1	2	3	4	5
12. The school facility has adequate instructional materials and audiovisual and technology equipment to support student learning and academic achievement.	1	2	3	4	5

(Continued)

Form 6.2   (Continued)

	Low				High
13. The school principal and teacher-leaders use school-level and classroom academic achievement data along with diverse teaching strategies to support students in their learning.	1	2	3	4	5
14. The school's management of programs is organized to maximize the use of instructional time dedicated to student academic achievement.	1	2	3	4	5
15. The school principal and teacher-leaders understand how to provide individual students with safety net services to prevent low performance, and the classroom teachers are aware of the various safety net services available to students at the school site and through district office services.	1	2	3	4	5
16. The school has adequate before-school and after-school childcare services.	1	2	3	4	5
17. The school has sufficient tutorial services, mentoring support, and career development counseling services available to students.	1	2	3	4	5
18. The school offers after-school enrichment activities, including performing arts activities, team sports, and activities clubs.	1	2	3	4	5
19. The school provides families with adequate health and human care services.	1	2	3	4	5
20. Parents are provided with parent education classes, including child development training and guidance in how to adequately support their children's academic performance.	1	2	3	4	5
21. The school provides parents with family literacy training.	1	2	3	4	5
22. The school provides English language learners with training to help their children achieve academic success in school.	1	2	3	4	5
23. The school provides service-learning opportunities for children and their families in schools.	1	2	3	4	5
24. The school provides families with counseling support services.	1	2	3	4	5
25. The school provides the school community with an extensive volunteer development program to support a school's classroom and administrative activities.	1	2	3	4	5

List the classroom teachers' and school's five primary needs for building community partnerships or for funding support:

1.

2.

(Continued)

Form 6.2   (Continued)

3.

4.

5.

List five strategies that will support or provide resources for these needs:

1.

2.

3.

4.

5.

Once a school's staff identifies and prioritizes its needs and its teachers' needs, the principal can invite stakeholders to match their resources to the needs of the school. A community partner can be asked to provide (a) a description of its services for the school; (b) a summary of the organization's background, expertise, and capacity to deliver needed services; (c) a budget highlighting costs of various services; and (d) a fundraising plan of how the organization will leverage funding to meet the needs of the school (Burke, 2002). After receiving various stakeholder proposals for specific services, the principal and teacher-leaders can review each community organization's proposed program to determine its feasibility and cost-effectiveness. Sometimes the principal and teacher-leaders will find that a community organization can provide extensive services at a more affordable cost than the school's internal delivery system. Examples of effective

Form 6.3   Sample Prospective Funder Worksheet

Directions: List the various program components that have been identified as needs for a teacher's classroom or for the school. In the space provided, list various funding sources or partnerships that can be formed for providing or funding prioritized school activities or school-based programs.

Primary Program Needs	Potential Partnerships and Funding Sources
1.	List three prospective partners that can service this need: 1.1 1.2 1.3 List three funding sources who can fund or provide added resources: 1.4 1.5 1.6
2.	List three prospective partners that can service this need: 2.1 2.2 2.3 List three funding sources who can fund or provide added resources: 2.4

(Continued)

Form 6.3   (Continued)

Primary Program Needs	Potential Partnerships and Funding Sources
	2.5
	2.6
3.	List three prospective partners that can service this need:
	3.1
	3.2
	3.3
	List three funding sources who can fund or provide added resources:
	3.4
	3.5
	3.6
4.	List three prospective partners that can service this need:
	4.1
	4.2
	4.3
	List three funding sources who can fund or provide added resources:
	4.4
	4.5
	4.6

subcontract partnerships and community donations for a school include

- Nutritional breakfasts, lunches, and afterschool snacks for an extended childcare program provided by a local catering business.
- Before- and afterschool childcare provided by a child development agency.
- Computer equipment and troubleshooting services provided by a local technology business for use in the classrooms and for an extended childcare program.
- Books donated by a used bookstore for a kindergarten's family literacy training program.
- Afterschool tutorial services provided by AmeriCorps volunteers.
- Afterschool sports teams managed on site by the YMCA, Boys and Girls Club, or Police Athletic League.
- Performing arts activities provided by a local theater group and a museum docent program.
- A physical fitness program with age-appropriate activities provided by the local college athletics department.
- School uniforms for low-income families donated by a local clothing manufacturer.

School business ventures involve true partnerships in that both parties are equal and each party will derive specific benefits from contracts, sponsorships, or donations. Whenever a school's principal and teacher-leaders delegate program responsibilities and contracts to other groups, the teachers and administrators have more time and money to focus on the academic growth and training of diverse student groups. Form 6.4 provides a sample worksheet that a principal and teacher-leaders can use to review each community organization's proposed program to determine its feasibility and cost-effectiveness.

Form 6.4   Sample Review Form for Prospective Service
Contractors

Directions: Complete the information below for each prospective
service contractor or funder of each of the prioritized needs
identified in the needs assessment.

Primary Program Needs	*Service Contractor's Description of Services*
1.	1.1 Description of services: 1.2 Summary of organizational expertise: 1.3 Budget for services: 1.4 Organization's fundraising plan for leveraging added resources to meet the school needs:
2.	2.1 Description of services: 2.2 Summary of organizational expertise: 2.3 Budget for services: 2.4 Organization's fundraising plan for leveraging added resources to meet the school needs:
3.	3.1 Description of services: 3.2 Summary of organizational expertise: 3.3 Budget for services:

(Continued)

Form 6.4   (Continued)

Primary Program Needs	Service Contractor's Description of Services
	3.4 Organization's fundraising plan for leveraging added resources to meet the school needs:
4.	4.1 Description of services:
	4.2 Summary of organizational expertise:
	4.3 Budget for services:
	4.4 Organization's fundraising plan for leveraging added resources to meet the school needs:

CREATING A STRATEGIC PLAN
FOR AGGRESSIVE GRANT DEVELOPMENT

Creating a strategic plan for aggressive grant development can leverage diverse funding to meet funders' requirements and grant implementation limitations (Burke & Liljenstolpe, 1993). Once the school site principal and teacher-leaders are clear about their priorities and have identified prospective subcontractors for various services, the school principal can create a matrix of funding options that can help him or her determine what programs should be funded by various funding sources. For example, a before- and afterschool childcare center managed by a subcontracted childcare business can be supported by federal afterschool funding provided through the state. The childcare program can also be funded through federal job-training funding for low-income families managed by the county office of education.

Form 6.5   Sample Matrix of Funding Options for School-Site
Subcontract Services

Directions: List each prioritized need. Check the funding source a
service provider has available for funding the service or program
at the school site. If the service is fully funded, check that it is an
expanded service.

Need	Federal	State	County	Local	Donations	Sponsor	Expanded Services
1.							
2.							
3.							
4.							
5.							

An afterschool sports program provided by the YMCA at the school site can be coordinated by the after-school childcare subcontractor. Funding for the program may already be provided to the YMCA through ongoing community development resources. Added funding can be obtained to purchase uniforms for the students playing on teams. A contracted donation for team uniforms can be obtained from a local garment manufacturer. After existing funding sources are identified, a matrix of funding options can indicate which programs will require future resource development for sustained funding or new funding. Form 6.5 provides a sample matrix of funding options for proposed subcontract services.

Conclusion

When considering the six reform steps utilized by the Compton Unified School District and other national schools struggling to overcome low performance, the key results accountability process continues to generate increased results after a decade from initial implementation. Effective succession management or the ongoing planning for transitions is an integral component of the key results accountability process. The following 10 succession management strategies can contribute to sustained results:

1. **Develop a support team** of school-site principals, teachers, and clerical staff who have the essential skills to create policies and procedures that ensure adequate accountability for tracking student achievement and fiscal controls to manage resources.

2. **Recruit central office and school-site administrators** who will commit to the long-term institutional changes required for increasing student achievement and stabilizing and securing resources to support key results reform strategies.

3. **Create facilities that will support a safe and secure environment for students** that can in turn foster the cultural changes required for student growth and achievement within their school community.

4. **Train and provide staff with the leadership skills required** to sustain institutionalized changes and offer

them the technological tools and skills to institutionalize those changes.

5. **Create an in-house teacher-credentialing program** to ensure an adequate supply of trained and committed teachers to reduce teacher turnover in urbanized and economically challenged school environments.

6. **Organize summer principal institutes** that build camaraderie among principals and provide the essential skills required for leadership change and development.

7. **Create ongoing school-site training for leadership development** that supports the key results accountability system.

8. **Provide ongoing districtwide literacy training** to ensure all teachers and support staff can adequately train students in the literacy curriculum while considering the individualized learning needs of economically challenged students, ESL students, and students identified as having special needs.

9. **Create an attendance tracking system** at each school site that can adequately support the attendance of all students and build a safety net of support services to ensure that families of students with excessive absences receive adequate help to remedy the situation.

10. **Create a schedule of ongoing achievement testing** for each student to measure changes in performance and to ensure that students who demonstrate academic difficulties receive immediate and ongoing tutorial support and other safety net services.

Succession planning requires that school leaders consider whom they must hire to ensure the development of long-term and cohesive leadership teams at each school site. Young and impressionable school leaders may be very effective in sustaining institutional change in urbanized schools because they (a) are still idealistic about the favorable impact of their diligent efforts; (b) typically have less distractions in their personal life, still have flexible lifestyles, and can work longer hours; (c) typically have the time and energy required for institutionalized change; and (d) are highly motivated to make an impact on future career growth opportunities.

Passionate, well-trained, and experienced school principals and teacher-leaders can instill a professional code of ethics for all school personnel and teachers. These dedicated professionals are committed to the change process and can inspire other long-term employees to respond to the challenges of overcoming low performance. Examples of effective long-term school leaders include:

- A civics teacher with 30 years of classroom experience who treats all students with respect and maintains a student-centered classroom with student-generated work displayed on bulletin boards under subtitles of key concepts included in the course. The civics teacher summarizes key concepts at the beginning of each class session and engages the students in a dialogue about those concepts. Students complete group projects that reinforce key concepts during each class period. Class projects also include the skills required to conduct research at the college level. Students in the course are expected to perform at a high achievement level and are assured that they have the capacity to succeed in college.

- A school-site secretary who has lived in the community all of her life and who is anxious to make the changes required to adequately support the needs of the school's low-performing students. Although she has limited computer literacy skills and plans to retire from the district in the next five years, she works overtime without compensation to learn the skills essential for mastering the computer. Through her commitment to change, she is very effective in supporting school accountability implementation for sustained success. She is spiritually optimistic about the potential of overstressed students and their families as well as about the overall school's gains in an urbanized challenged community.

• A bright, young teacher who was promoted to a principal assignment and who demonstrates outstanding passion and work ethics. Her leadership inspires teachers to exceed traditional boundaries when serving students who have historically failed in school. A large percentage of the school's students come from foster homes, are highly transient, and display a broad array of learning challenges. The principal's commitment and an inspired teaching staff model a caring concern for student success. The school leadership team is also instrumental in leveraging diverse safety net services to ensure added student achievement.

• An experienced school principal who attended the same urban middle school and who inspires the students with his committed leadership in bringing community services and resources to the school and its neighboring community. The passionate principal tackles students' low academic performance with extensive afterschool tutorial programs. He is effective in recruiting the local sheriffs to participate in school-site gang abatement programs and mentoring for at-risk youth.

• A seasoned central office leader who spends countless hours creating engaging staff development sessions to increase a principal's and school leadership team's effectiveness. The importance of the key results accountability system is embraced in all staff development activities. At one staff development session, the district leader was able to educate and recruit other district administrators, school leaders, community leaders, and the neighboring school community to participate in a school community cultural event that included extensive literacy development activities for students and their families.

• A central office administrator who creates the internal financial policies required for careful financial planning at school sites and for increased resources to meet individualized student needs. The administrator also streamlines the purchasing functions to ensure that teachers and students receive program services and supplies in a timely manner. Principals are provided with timelines of when to submit purchase orders to ensure that annual expenditures are maximized for securing resources. Capital expenditures and service contracts are carefully managed to ensure that a school's facilities are adequately prepared to meet the growth needs of its student population.

As students and their families become confident that a school principal and teachers are dedicated to meeting students' individualized learning needs, they become committed to supporting the key results accountability process. For example, committed middle school students participate in a school's safety net programs, which include a college preparation tutorial and mentoring program, an afterschool remedial reading program, a math tutorial program, an afterschool sports program, and an afterschool community service program. Committed parents of these students attend college education nights at the school to learn about the subject selections required for state college and university acceptance. The school's leadership team also teaches parents how to support their children in their homework and how families can provide extracurricular experiences that enhance academic learning. The school's counselor provides committed parents with parent education classes about how to access school services and how to effectively nurture their child's overall emotional, social, physical, spiritual, and academic growth.

Principals, school leaders, school support staff, parents, and students who support key results accountability are clear about the purpose of education in meeting the academic needs of all students. These stakeholder groups can effectively infuse this core value into a school's policies, procedures, and trainings to sustain the key results process.

Resource: The Results-Based Intervention for School Efficacy (RISE) Project

The Results-Based Intervention for School Efficacy (RISE) case study was initially conceived as a response to the complex needs of low-performing schools in California. Project RISE provides the support infrastructure for short-term crisis management and long-term capacity building in public schools and school districts in turmoil. The partnerships and services of universities, foundations, businesses, and private entities are also utilized to support K–12 urban schools in crisis. Many of the effective leadership strategies and reform practices utilized in the project are effective in helping schools and districts improve the overall achievement of their students, teaching staff, and operational practices. Project RISE uses a crisis-response-team approach to facilitate the implementation of a corrective action plan that benchmarks progress through a Key Results Recovery Matrix.

Project RISE advocates a comprehensive state intervention structure for best practices in state takeovers and schools in crisis. The RISE team provides a technical support mechanism for the state board of education, the superintendent of public instruction, and the state legislature in the assumption of legal rights, duties, and powers of the governing board of schools that do not meet their growth target. Project RISE may also serve local governing boards for any individual school or school district experiencing any sort of academic or management crisis.

The mission of Project RISE is to institute and document successful urban reforms that address urban realities to help all students achieve in reading, writing, and math in a safe, clean, and secure environment. The project's beliefs include the following:

- All students must reach benchmarked standards of achievement. No exception! No excuses!
- The standards must be the same for all students.
- Contribution to student performance is the only criteria for judging the merit of any activity that takes place at any level of the educational system.
- Assessment systems, the curriculum, the entire instructional program, the professional development program, and the accountability system must be linked at every level to the standards of student achievement.
- Good instruction is important, but it is not enough. Each student needs to know that school and district staffs care about him or her and that his or her success is achievable and important.
- The entire community must be involved and organized to support the students.
- Schools and district support staff must provide high performance and customer friendly workplaces.
- A school's staff must provide staff with the freedom, training, and motivation to make informed decisions as capable employees who are then held accountable for the results of their work.

Based on these beliefs, Project RISE focuses on the following six components:

1. Improving student achievement in the core subjects.

2. Aligning teaching and learning with student performance.

3. Linking professional development for all staff to the goals for students.

4. Providing safe, clean, and secure school facilities.

5. Increasing management effectiveness, efficiency, and accountability.

6. Forging stronger linkages with parents, families, and the community.

In developing the recovery plan for a low-performing school, assessments are conducted using legal and professional standards in five areas:

1. Pupil achievement

2. Facility management

3. Fiscal and budget management

4. Community relations

5. Personnel management

This implementation recovery plan is multifaceted and focuses on a school or district recovery, enhanced student achievement, and clear expected outcomes. The expectations for recovery must focus on classrooms and staff development as well as instructional support for staff that sets clear expectations through the development and implementation of standards-based key results. The RISE staff works collaboratively with schools and districts to implement effective, research-based best practices. The RISE staff offers ongoing coaching as well as professional development services and support for the systemic changes needed to implement effective school improvement programs.

Project RISE believes that if schools train, support, develop, and retain teachers to the best of their ability, and hold them to the highest standard for student achievement, the schools will be successful. It is the project's desire to invest in teachers and promote a long-term relationship between teachers and their schools. Project RISE can ensure a quality learning environment by instituting effective school planning, staff development, and resource allocation.

The RISE vision holds that, to teach effectively, stakeholders must use proven, results-based practices and comprehensive data assessment systems to make daily decisions about instruction and student achievement. To this end, Project RISE employs a school-based assessment system that tightly connects the instructional loop of teaching, testing, analyzing, and reteaching. Such a system must bring the power of data-driven decisions into the hands of all invested in the outcome: administrators, teachers, parents, and students.

Project RISE can work to employ curriculum and instructional strategies based on validated research from organizations such as the National Institute for Child Health and Human Development (NICHD). Project RISE can also help schools align program and instructional resources to the curriculum and provide student equity. The RISE team can help staff implement curriculum that will be differentiated by student need and that has assessment-driven instructional objectives. Student progress can be closely monitored with intervention programs in place to address the needs of the most at-risk students using both school and community resources. Project RISE can create a culture of achievement by helping schools hold students, teachers, and parents to rigorous academic standards and expectations. The project attempts to pursue small, important steps to make continuous progress toward ambitious goals. RISE makes an effort to involve parents, businesses, and the community in the success of their schools and the lives of their students, and to always put student learning as the first priority. The technical assistance role of the Project RISE staff in a school or a district recovery process must include the following critical components:

1. **RISE Teams:** The Project RISE response team is staffed by experts and experienced school reform practitioners who have clearly demonstrated success in the most difficult of urban circumstances. A core staff provides full-time technical assistance while other part-time consultants are used for the specific needs as designed in the recovery plans. Each RISE practitioner is capable of effectively assessing and facilitating the implementation of appropriate action plans for reaching and exceeding the required growth results. By tapping the expertise of professional educators throughout the state, each RISE response team is developed to serve as a support and networking unit for each of the six primary project components. The opportunities for professional growth for school and/or district stakeholders are crucial for any substantial and sustained change to occur.

2. **Implementation Facilitator:** The reform facilitator works hand in hand with a district's superintendent, board, staff, and other interested community individuals in the implementation of a recovery plan.

3. **Assessment Process:** The assessment process includes (a) an analysis of the individual school improvement plan; (b) an examination of each school's student achievement data; (c) a comparison of student work related to the state standards in reading, language, and math; (d) an audit of the curriculum and instructional strategies used to increase achievement; (e) the status of the present level and type of parent, community, business, and university support; (f) a budget analysis for optimal leverage; and (g) facility and personnel management reviews.

4. **Leadership Training/Coaching Program:** Low-performing, hard-to-staff schools need trained principals with

follow-up support coaching in the essential elements of instructional leadership. Training topics include, but are not limited to, the following:

- Instructional leadership and management strategies to use instructional technology to improve pupil performance
- Reading process, including phonetic knowledge, articulation, phonology, orthography, morphology, comprehension, active participation, and English language development strategies.
- Results-based classroom visitations
- English language learner compliance and quality instruction
- Special education preventive strategies that work
- Parents and the school community as partners
- Core academic standards
- Alignment of frameworks and instructional materials to support the state academic standards
- Assessment instruments, data, and school management technology to improve pupil performance
- School finance, facility, and personnel management

5. **Standards-Based Recovery System:** The recovery standards provide a whole-school approach for the full recovery of a school or district. The recovery system includes clearly defined measurable goals with benchmarks for meeting those goals. The system provides the continual tracking status of a reform strategy while building capacity for full implementation, as illustrated in Figure R.1.

To support instructional effectiveness, Project RISE's role in providing comprehensive professional development is critical. RISE's commitment to helping all children learn to the three R's is manifested in the professional development it can provide. RISE can build a culture of open communication among teachers and at all levels of the organization. All classrooms can have an open-door policy. Teachers can have more staff time for grade-level collaboration, frequent assessments,

Figure R.1   The Standards-Based Recovery System

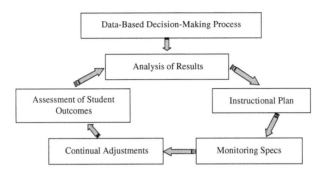

and action-oriented data analysis. Teachers can be trained with research-based strategies. Specialists and district trainers can be used to deliver professional development in addition to teaching and classroom support or coaching duties. Professional development time can include the following:

- Summer new-teacher preparation institutes with weeks of on-site training done by senior staff
- Bimonthly new-teacher training with professional reading circles and strategies training
- Bimonthly grade-level collaboration
- Monthly ongoing site staff management with core teachers sent to training and inservices
- Professional development days during which teachers learn how to plan and analyze assessments

6. **Key Results Classroom Quality Indicators Matrix:** Project RISE provides staff and school leaders with a classroom visitation assessment matrix based on promising instructional practices, including (a) effective lesson delivery, (b) writing assessments, (c) a student-centered environment, (d) quality lesson plans, (e) available instructional materials, (f) adequate test preparation, (g) safety nets, (h) instructional integrity, and (i) attendance accountability.

7. **Facility/Campus Grading System:** A nationally recognized criterion-based assessment of the physical plant is

provided by RISE that ensures health and safety compliance for an educationally conducive environment. The grading system also tracks and evaluates the responsiveness of the district maintenance request system.

8. **Documenting and Honoring Student Success:** Project RISE has a proven track record of supporting schools and districts in crisis. Currently, little research exists that provides the necessary direction and guidance regarding a state's control of a school district. There are few proven strategies that effectively support a school district's process to return governance responsibilities to local school boards. Historically, the only guidance available to schools and districts in crisis has come directly from state legislators rather than trained and empowered educators, community members, or university entities.

The tables on the next few pages provide examples of how the RISE Project can support a school or district recovery process for supporting successful student achievement. Table R.1 outlines the roles school members, district staff, and community partners must play in helping a low-performing school develop a recovery plan. Table R.2 identifies the various types of technical assistance activities available through the project, and Table R.3 describes effective strategies for improving school efficacy. Table R.4 provides a sample RISE workplan, including goals, activities, a timeline, and an evaluation to support a school's and/or district's recovery.

UNDERSTANDING THE LEGISLATIVE BACKGROUND FOR PROJECT RISE

California and 24 other states have developed takeover legislation allowing school districts to be placed under state receivership. Emeryville, California, Philadelphia, Pennsylvania, Detroit, Michigan, and others are part of a growing list of school districts in crisis. The state of California and other states are experiencing a crisis in facilitating the learning development

Table R.1   School and District Role With Partners to Develop the
Recovery Plan

Project Partners	Description of Role
District representatives	District staff will assist with the needed technical support to accomplish a schoolwide assessment and evaluation process.
Individual schools	School leadership teams, school-site councils, school-site classified staff, and certificated staff will participate in all program implementation, site assessments, and evaluation processes.
School families	School families will participate in professional development activities, contribute to the governance process, assist in all levels of planning and implementation, and provide increased representation on the school leadership team to enhance parental support at home.
Community members	Community outreach programs will recruit community support; train, screen, and maintain community volunteers; focus on at-risk students and families; and organize celebrations and cultural events to enhance community-school connections.
Local agencies	Local agencies will provide input at school meetings as well as at the school forums. These agencies will work with the district staff in coordinating and streamlining the delivery of services at various sites.

and achievement of millions of pupils in the states' public schools. The RISE project provides California—and can provide the twenty-four other states that have developed takeover legislation—technical support they need to improve.

In California, the California Department of Education (CDE) is responsible for the administration of the enactment

Table R.2   Description of Technical Assistance Activities

Activity	Description
Needs assessment	Project RISE staff and district staff will assist schools in compiling school data and in designing efficient processes for tracking and collecting data on select promising practices.
Aligning school goals	Project RISE staff will assist in meeting district and school goals and aligning them with state standards.
Coordination of curriculum and instruction	Project RISE staff and the district staff will facilitate the alignment of the school curriculum and instructional program with the state standards and will work to meet the requirements set by the state for special needs students and English language learners.
Leveraging and managing school budgets	Project RISE staff will assist school staff in implementing school budgets that allow for optimal use and leveraging of available school resources. The district staff will maintain a financial reporting system that complies with grant requirements.
Development of school-based information systems	Project RISE staff will work collaboratively with district research staff to create a school-based information tracking system. If needed, an independent contractor will be hired to design an appropriate tracking model.
Development of a school's accountability system	Project RISE staff and the district staff will collaboratively create the template and provide the technical assistance for developing a school accountability system.

(Continued)

Table R.2   Continued)

Activity	Description
Coordination of professional development	The district's professional development department will coordinate with Project RISE staff to support the recovery plan.
Development of the public engagement process	Project RISE staff and the district staff will coordinate a districtwide or school-based public engagement process as needed to support the recovery plan. Through an evaluation, the school-site staff will conduct needs assessments, organize community forums, and inform the community about the recovery progress.
Facility management process	The district staff will assist Project RISE staff in ensuring the maintenance of the school's educational facility to provide an environment conducive to learning.

of the 1999 Public Schools Accountability Act (PSAA). Its three major provisions include (1) evaluating the Academic Performance Index (API) of individual schools; (2) administering the Immediate Intervention/Underperforming School Program (II/USP) to assist low-performing schools to improve student academic performance; and (3) providing awards and incentives to schools for increasing student academic performance measured by the API through the Governor's Performance Awards (Padia, 2001).

When reviewing the initial results of the II/USP, the CDE has focused its evaluation on the first cohort of 430 II/USP schools funded during the 1999–2000 school year. Funding for this program includes II/USP state money to support a two-stage process of planning and implementing an action plan over three years. Federal funds are provided for individual Comprehensive School Reform Demonstration (CSRD) projects that support a school's use of a research-based school reform model over a three-year period. The II/USP cohort of

Table R.3   Strategies for Improving School Efficacy

Strategy	Barrier Removal or School Efficacy
Cluster Project RISE schools under one leader for effectiveness	Clustering will facilitate communication on program implementation and maximize student performance and district support. Extensive longitudinal data can be compiled within the Project RISE family.
Incorporate each school plan into a district reform model	A district reform model can be designed that streamlines the school's need for change through a centralized technical support mechanism.
Include union leadership in Project RISE activities	The district will facilitate effective strategies for working with classified and certificated union leadership to support recovery efforts.
Involve parents and community groups in program implementation	Project RISE staff and the school staff will effectively facilitate the use of the skills and resources of various community stakeholders for program implementation. This allows for ongoing community input, effective resource utilization, and community support.
Coordinate communication of individual components	The district will utilize the school's report cards, district publications, and the district's Web site for continuous updates to the community on the project's progress.
Coordinate each school's needs assessment, data collection, training, and evaluation	The district will provide each school with coordinated services from the appropriate departments to support the development, implementation, and evaluation of the recovery plans. This support can streamline services and provide process support coordinated through Project RISE.

Table R.4   Project RISE Workplan for School Reform

Goals and Activities	Time	Evaluation
Goal #1: To build organizational and leadership capacity through response teams and an implementation facilitator.		
• Create a school or district plan that integrates an appropriate best practices model for schoolwide improvement.	Fall	The plan will demonstrate an appropriate best practice model based on student data.
• Provide staff development at all levels to support the reform model.	Winter	80% of the trained executive staff, principals, and teachers will demonstrate increased knowledge.
• Statistically analyze effective school reform efforts.	Spring	A long-term plan will be developed that includes statistically analyzed reform efforts.
• Create comprehensive strategies for systemic change.	Summer	A long-term plan will be developed that includes comprehensive strategies for reform.
Goal #2: To provide curriculum and instructional support using a Key Results Recovery Matrix.		
• Use data to improve student test scores at the 5% growth target and increase effective teaching strategies.	Fall	The data-driven document will include strategies for student performance and teaching.
• Address the academic needs of diverse student learners.	Fall	The plan will include strategies for diverse learners.
• Align classroom content and standards (e.g., by using backloading).	Fall	Class content will align with standards.

(Continued)

Table R.4   (Continued)

Goals and Activities	Time	Evaluation
• Create effective classroom management strategies.	Fall	80% of teachers will demonstrate effective classroom management and instructional delivery strategies.
• Coach principals and teachers as instructional leaders.	Fall	80% of principals and teachers will demonstrate increased instructional leadership skills in coaching sessions.
• Integrate test preparation in content areas.	Winter	80% of teachers will integrate test preparation in content.
• Develop authentic student evaluations.	Winter	80% of teachers will collect authentic student evaluations.
• Develop grade-level structured lesson plans with project-based learning.	Spring	80% of teachers will include project-based learning in their lessons.
Goal #3: To provide financial, personnel, grantwriting, community outreach, and facilities support.		
• Provide schoolwide focus on school and community development.	Winter	80% of schools will demonstrate an increase in school and community partnerships.
• Develop astute business practices in financial management and acquisition of resources.	Fall	The district will reduce its audit findings by 50%, increase its grant development, and streamline service delivery.
• Develop a facility management evaluation process to ensure a quality environment.	Ongoing	School teams will monitor and facilitate facility corrections and beautification.

state and federal funded programs were evaluated using the following data sources (Padia, 2001):

- CDE database school profiles, including demographic attributes, student achievement, and API progress data
- Site visits to 25 II/USP schools, 12 state-funded II/USP planning schools, and 13 federally funded CSRD schools
- Surveys from II/USP school personnel

The CDE summarized the following evaluation results in a May 22, 2001 "Research Summary about Underperforming Schools" memorandum from William L. Padia, Division of Policy and Evaluation Director:

- The 430 II/USP schools in Cohort 1 constitute almost 13% of all API Deciles 1 through 5 schools in the 1999–2000 school year.
- Among the 350 state-funded II/USP planning schools, 62% had API schools in the Deciles 3 through 5.
- The 80 federally funded CSRD schools tend to be more concentrated in API Deciles 1 and 2.
- The data indicate that CSRD schools tend to have larger percentages of English language learners compared to the II/USP schools.
- An analysis of the CSRD school data further indicates that 83% of the students tested received Title I services and were designated as having low socioeconomic status.
- The external evaluators received high marks for acting as facilitators for the action plan process, involving parents and the community, and providing guidance and structure for the planning process.
- Criticisms of external evaluators included occasional mismatches, lack of accessibility and familiarity of the process, and a lack of experience with the school site and systematic school reform process.

Based on these preliminary results, the CDE concluded that the capacity of II/USP schools for change beyond the planning year is uncertain. In its analysis of the CSRD schools, the CDE stated that overall there is greater school choice and staff buy-in for reform. In summary, the CDE recommended the following for each type of funding (Padia, 2001):

- Schools selected by the state for II/USP participation should sign a buy-in agreement, and their districts must screen external evaluators that appear most appropriate from the state list.
- The CSRD schools must carefully select their CSRD model and the implementation process must ensure fidelity to the model design.

All participating schools must cooperate fully with the CDE statewide monitoring and evaluating activities in accordance with the II/USP local evaluation requirements of the PSAA law. The CDE policy and practices are serving as a model for other states as they struggle to identify effective strategies for serving the challenging needs of low-performing students. When considering the initial results of the II/USP program and the implications of the law, it mandates that the state superintendent of public instruction (SPI) shall assume all legal rights, duties, and powers of the governing board with respect to schools that fail to meet their 5% growth target (Padia, 2001). The CDE estimates that as many as 140 of the first cohort of II/USP schools could face state sanctions. Under the supervision of the state superintendent of instruction, (a) the management of a low-performing school can be assigned to a college, university, county office of education, or other appropriate educational institution; (b) the attendance options can be revised; (c) the school site can be changed to a charter school; (d) the certificated school employees can be reassigned; (e) a new collective bargaining agreement can be negotiated; or (f) the school can be reorganized or closed (Padia, 2001).

Assembly Bill 961 (AB961) is the 2001 High-Priority Grant Program that creates intermediate interventions as an option for the California State Board of Education (CSBE) and keeps the sanctions the same as the current law except after the third implementation year. The intermediate interventions give the CSBE the option to require local districts to contract with a school assistance intervention team to monitor and report to the local board and state at least three times a year (Padia, 2001).

References

Anderson, K. (1981). *Cutting deals with unlikely allies: An unorthodox approach to playing the political game.* Berkeley, CA: Anderson Negotiations/Communications Press.

Aronson, M. M. (1995). *Building communication partnerships with parents.* Westminster, CA: Teacher Created Materials.

Blakely, E. J. (1997). A new role for education in economic development: Tomorrow's economy today. *Education and Urban Society, 29*(4), 509–523.

Burke, M. A. (1999). Analyzing the cost effectiveness of using parents and community volunteers to improve students' language arts test scores (Doctoral dissertation, University of Southern California, 1999). *Dissertation Abstracts International, A60/06,* Z1915.

Burke, M. A. (2002). *Simplified grantwriting.* Thousand Oaks, CA: Corwin.

Burke, M. A., Baca, R., Picus, L. O., & Jones, C. E. (2003). *Leveraging resources for student success: How school leaders build equity.* Thousand Oaks, CA: Corwin.

Burke, M. A., & Liljenstolpe, C. (1993). *Creative fund-raising: A guide for success.* Menlo Park, CA: Crisp.

Burke, M. A., & Picus, L. O. (2001). *Developing community-empowered schools.* Thousand Oaks, CA: Corwin.

Comer, J. P., Ben-Avie, M., Haynes, N. M., & Joyner, E. T. (1999). *Child by child: The Comer process for change in education.* New York, NY: Teachers College Press.

Compton Unified School District. (1999). *Volunteers in public schools (VIPS) handbook: Training materials for school site implementation.* Compton, CA: Author.

Compton Unified School District School Operations. (2000). *Key results visitation team training.* Compton, CA: Author.

Compton Unified School District Research, Evaluation, and Assessment. (2001). *Key results indicators and final weighted average score.* Compton, CA: Author.

Curriculum Development and Supplemental Materials Commission. (2000). *Mathematics framework for California public schools: Kindergarten through Grade Twelve.* Sacramento, CA: California Department of Education.

Curriculum Management Audit Centers. (2000). *Maximizing student achievement: Curriculum and assessment design and delivery—Level 1.* Huxley, IA: Author.

Englert, R. M. (1993). Understanding the urban context and conditions of practice of school administration. In P. B. Forsyth & M. Tollerico (Eds.), *City schools: Leading the way* (pp. 1–63). Thousand Oaks, CA: Corwin.

English, F. W. (1992). *Deciding what to teach and test: Developing, aligning, and auditing the curriculum.* Thousand Oaks, CA: Corwin.

Epstein, J. L. (2001). *School, family, and community partnerships.* Boulder, CA: Westview.

Epstein, J. L., Coates, L., Salinas, K. C., Sanders, M. G., & Simon, B. S. (1997). *School, family and community partnerships: Your handbook for action.* Thousand Oaks, CA: Corwin.

Fields Devereaux Architects & Engineers. (2001). *Compton Unified School District comprehensive facilities master plan.* Compton, CA: Author.

Fiore, D. J. (2002). *School community relations.* Larchmont, NY: Eye on Education.

Forester, E. M. (1996). *State intervention in local school districts: Educational solution or political process?* Paper presented at the annual meeting of the American Educational Research Association, New York, NY.

Fullan, M. (1993). *Changing forces: Probing the depths of educational reform.* London, England: Flamer.

Kerchner, C. T. (1997). Education as a city's big industry. *Education and Urban Society, 29*(4), 424–441.

King, C. S., & Stivers, C. (1998). *Government is us.* Thousand Oaks, CA: Sage.

Kritek, W. J. (1993). Effective change in urban schools. In P. B. Forsyth & M. Tollerico (Eds.), *City schools: Leading the way* (pp. 253–286). Thousand Oaks, CA: Corwin.

Lester, J. P., & Stewart, J., Jr. (2000). *Public policy: An evolutionary approach.* Belmont, CA: Wadsworth.

Levin, H. M., & McEwan, H. M. (2001). *Cost-effectiveness analysis.* Thousand Oaks, CA: Corwin.

Lindsey, R. B., Robins, K. R., & Terrell, R. D. (1999). *Cultural proficiency: A manual for school leaders.* Thousand Oaks, CA: Corwin.

Murphy, L. (2000, Fall). Compton district resolves civil rights complaints. *WestEd Equity News,* 1–5.

Oakes, J., Quartz, K. H., Ryan, S., & Lipton, M. (2000). *Becoming good American schools: The struggle for civic virtue in education reform.* San Francisco, CA: Jossey-Bass.

Padia, W. L. (2001). *Research summary about low-performing schools.* Sacramento, CA: California Department of Education.

Parker, L. (1993). Acquiring and using resources. In P. B. Forsyth & M. Tollerico (Eds.), *City schools: Leading the way* (pp. 1–63). Thousand Oaks, CA: Corwin.

Ramsey, R. D. (2001). *Fiscal fitness for school administrators: How to stretch resources and do even more with less.* Thousand Oaks, CA: Corwin.

Reeves, D. B. (2000). *Accountability action: A blueprint for learning organizations.* Denver, CO: Advanced Learning Centers.

Sanders, E. T. W. (1999). *Urban school leadership: Issues and strategies.* Larchmont, NY: Eye on Education.

Short, P. J., & Greer, J. T. (1997). *Leadership in empowered schools.* Upper Saddle River, NJ: Prentice Hall.

Spring, J. (2000). *American education.* Boston, MA: McGraw-Hill.

Stanton-Salazar, R. D. (2001). *Manufacturing hope and despair: The school and kin support networks of U.S.–Mexican youth.* NY: Teachers College Press.

Suggested Readings

Ballen, J., Casey, J. C., & de Kanter, A. (1998). *The corporate imperative: Results and benefits of business involvement in education.* Washington, DC: U.S. Department of Education.

Banks, J. A. (1997). *Educating citizens in a multicultural society.* New York: Teachers College Press.

Bennis, W., & Goldsmith, J. (1997). *Learning to lead.* Reading, MA: Addison-Wesley.

Boethel, M. (1999). Service learning: A strategy for rural school improvement and community revitalization. *Benefits 2*(2), 1–6. Austin TX: Southwest Educational Laboratory.

Burtless, G. (1996). Introduction and Summary. In G. Burtless (Ed.), *Does money matter?: The effect of school resources on student achievement and adult success* (pp. 1–42). Washington, DC: The Brookings Institution.

California Department of Education. (1992). *Alternative approaches to assessment and evaluation in family English literacy programs.* Sacramento, CA: The California Department of Education.

Edelman, M. W. (1999). *Lanterns.* Boston: Beacon.

Fitzgerald, J. (1997). Linking school-to-work programs to community economic development in urban schools. *Urban Education, 32*(4), 489–511.

Freire, P. (1985). *The politics of education: Culture, power, and education.* South Hadley, MA: Bergin and Garvey.

Gordon, E. W. (1999). *Education and justice: A view from the back of the bus.* New York: Teachers College Press.

Hanuschek, E. A. (1994). *Making schools work: Improving performance and controlling costs.* Washington, DC: The Brookings Institution.

Hutson, H. M., Jr. (1981). Inservice best practices: The learnings of general education. *Journal of Research and Development in Education, 14,* 1–9.

Jennings, J. F. (Ed.). (1995). *National issues in education: Goals 2000 and school-to-work.* Washington, DC: The Institute for Educational Leadership.

Joyce, B., & Showers, B. (1980). Improving inservice training: The messages of research. *Educational Leadership, 37,* 379–385.

Karasoff, P. (1999). Opening the door to collaborative practice. *Teacher Education Quarterly, 26*(4), 53–67.

Ladd, H. F. (1996). Introduction. In H. F. Ladd (Ed.), *Holding schools accountable: Performance-based reform in education* (pp. 1–19). Washington, DC: The Brookings Institution.

MacKinnon, B. (2001). *Ethics: Theory and contemporary issues.* Belmont, CA: Wadsworth.

McLemore, S. D., & Romo, H. D. (1998). *Racial and ethnic relations in America* (5th ed.). Boston: Allyn & Bacon.

National Commission on Excellence and Equity in Education. (1983). *A nation at risk: The imperative of educational reform.* Washington, DC: U.S. Department of Education.

Olsen, L., Chang, H., De La Rosa Salazar, D., Leong, C., McCall Perez, Z., McClain, G., & Raffel, L. (1994). *The unfinished journey: Restructuring schools in a diverse society.* San Francisco: California Tomorrow.

Orfield, G., Eaton, S., & the Harvard Project on School Desegregation. (1996). *Dismantling desegregation: The quiet reversal of Brown verses Board of Education.* NY: The New Press.

Sweeney, J., Schenirer, J., & Lefkovitz, B. (2001). Developing results-based school/community partnerships. *Journal for the Community Approach, 2*(1), 4–8.

U. S. Department of Education. (1994). *Strong families, strong schools: Building community partnerships for learning.* Washington, DC: Author.

WestEd. (1996). *School reform: A new outlook.* San Francisco: Author.

Wolf, S. (1983). Ethics, legal ethics, and the ethics of law. In D. Luban (Ed.), *The good lawyer* (pp. 41–49). Lanham, MD: Rowan & Littlefield.

Index

**CORWIN
PRESS**

The Corwin Press logo—a raven striding across an open book— represents the union of courage and learning. Corwin Press is committed to improving education for all learners by publishing books and other professional development resources for those serving the field of K–12 education. By providing practical, hands-on materials, Corwin Press continues to carry out the promise of its motto: "**Helping Educators Do Their Work Better.**"